AMERICAN POETS PROJECT

The American Poets Project
is published with a gift in memory of
JAMES MERRILL

Karl Shapiro

selected poems

john updike editor

AMERICAN POETS PROJECT

THE LIBRARY OF AMERICA

The paper used in this publication meets the minimum requirements of the American National Standard for Information Sciences—Permanence of Paper for Printed Library Materials, ANSI Z39.48—1984.

Design by Chip Kidd and Mark Melnick.
Frontispiece courtesy Sophie Wilkins Shapiro.

Library of Congress Cataloging-in-Publication Data:
Shapiro, Karl Jay, 1913–2000
    [Poems. Selections]
    Selected poems / Karl Shapiro ; John Updike, editor.
        p. cm. — (American poets project ; 3)
    Includes index.
        I. Updike, John. II. Title. III. Series
PS3537.H27 A6 2003
811'.52 — dc21
2002032123

10 9 8 7 6 5 4 3 2 1

Karl
Shapiro

CONTENTS

INTRODUCTION

Karl Jay Shapiro was born in Baltimore in 1913; when he was drafted into the peacetime army, in March of 1941, he was no teenage conscript but a twenty-seven-year-old man whose poetic vocation was already well developed. His poems were appearing in *Poetry* and *Partisan Review*, and on the eve of his shipping out to Australia in 1942 (on the *Queen Mary* painted gray as a troopship), he had arranged with Reynal & Hitchcock for his first commercially published collection, *Person, Place and Thing*. This was not his first appearance between hard covers. In 1935 his father and uncle had arranged, through a medical textbook company, for a volume, *Poems*, to be privately printed by The Waverly Press in Baltimore—an event sardonically recalled in "Recapitulations," number V. In 1941, twenty-one of his poems, under the laconic overall title "Noun," represented him in *Five Young American Poets*, the second of a New Directions series. *Person, Place and Thing* appeared in 1942, though a year was to pass before he saw a copy;

it won warm reviews* and *Poetry*'s Levinson Prize. While stationed in Australia, he became the friend and lover of Cecily Crozier, the editor of the literary magazine *A Comment*; his brisk, revelatory memoir of his youth, *The Younger Son*, disguised her as "Bonamy Quorn." She published for him, in 1942, in Melbourne, a new collection, *The Place of Love*, containing poems of his and fragments of the letters they exchanged when his military duties separated them. He was in the Medical Corps, and saw most of his action in New Guinea. In his three years overseas, under what his introduction called "the peculiarly enlivening circumstances of soldiering," he composed most of the content of *V-Letter and Other Poems* (1944) and all of the 2,030-line verse *Essay on Rime* (1945). *V-Letter*, edited and arranged by his agent and future first wife, Evalyn Katz, won the 1945 Pulitzer Prize for Poetry.

While still a soldier, Shapiro had already achieved some celebrity back in the States as "a kind of phenomenon, a poet in the Battle Zone." Honors awaited him in peacetime America. He served in 1946-47 as the Consultant in Poetry at the Library of Congress, a post now dignified as Poet Laureate. In 1947 he was named an associate professor at Johns Hopkins, though his own forays into higher education had never quite won him a college degree. He left that job in 1950 to edit *Poetry* in Chicago; in 1956 he became professor at the University of Nebraska and the editor of *Prairie Schooner*. From 1966 to 1968 he taught at the Circle Campus of the University of Illinois in Chicago and from 1968 to 1985 at the University of California at Davis.

* "His is on all grounds the finest young American talent to appear in many seasons"—Louise Bogan in *The New Yorker*. "A book which everyone interested in modern poetry ought to read"—Delmore Schwartz in *The Nation*.

His reputation, to some extent, went west with him; Robert Lowell and Elizabeth Bishop became the favored poets of his generation, and though Shapiro won the Bollingen Prize in 1968 the award was shared with John Berryman. Impolitically, he published criticism of his peers, beginning with *Essay on Rime*. "Nothing is more perilous to a poet's reputation than indulgence in criticism," he wrote in *The Younger Son*, but "he* didn't see any point in keeping mum about anything so important as his opinion." His publication, in 1964, of *The Bourgeois Poet*, consisting entirely of untitled, aggressively personal, and frequently sardonic prose poems, seemed almost an abdication, alienating readers who had admired his mastery and variety of metrical form. In later verse he wryly noted that "My Fame's Not Feeling Well" and registered his irritation at such a slight as his being dropped from the 1976 edition of *The Oxford Book of American Verse*, having been amply represented in the 1950 edition ("On Being Yanked from a Favorite Anthology").[†] With his third wife, the translator Sophie Wilkins,[‡] Shapiro returned to the eastern United States in 1994, and he lived on New York City's Upper West Side until his death in the year 2000.

* Writing in the 1980s, Shapiro follows Norman Mailer's example and speaks of himself in the third person, as "the poet."

† The 1950 edition was edited by F. O. Matthiessen, to whom Shapiro dedicated a collection and addressed a heroic poem on the anniversary of the critic's suicide; the 1976 edition was edited by the critic and Joyce biographer Richard Ellmann, who in "On Being Yanked . . ." appears as an "antisemitic Jew," a "text-louse, pilpulistic Joycean cockroach," and a "whore."

‡ His second wife, Teri Kovach Baldwin, whom he had married in the year, 1967, of his divorce from Evalyn Katz, died in 1982. Shapiro remarried in 1985.

His habits of mind were restless and contrarian. The originality, charm, and power of his early poems lie in their eagerness to render aspects of American experience never before given the dignity of a high rhetoric. Shapiro came to poetry in the wake of his more academically gifted older brother, Irvin; he grew up overhearing Irvin's conversations with his intellectual friends and prowling through the large number of books that came into the house by way of overflow from his father's moving and storage business, which included appropriation of unclaimed lots. The younger son read Poe, Baltimore's own in his last years, and Whitman, and late Victorians like Coventry Patmore and Charles Algernon Swinburne, whose long lines haunted Karl Shapiro's verse into his maturity; he was perhaps the last modern poet with an appetite and a flair for anapestic meter. The poems in his first, privately published volume include quaintly crabbed love sonnets, Shakespearean rather than Petrarchan in form; a rondeau, a triolet, a villanelle; verses of an antiquarian quaintness ("Gladdith! thy flag aflaunt/Thou lusty Troynovaunt!"); and then, after this elaborate Georgian sickliness, spare free verse thin and clipped on the page, imitating E. E. Cummings and William Carlos Williams.

Williams was his first living examplar; he sent the Rutherford doctor a copy of his book and Williams responded with "a long reply, a warm, friendly, encouraging greeting that said nothing about the quality of the poems." Shapiro, in *The Younger Son*, praises Williams as his favorite American poet, though he cannot be, he says, a Williams disciple. The doctor-poet, in his Rutherford domain, functioned as "an authority and a savior and a cop, a force in the little town," and his minimal, direct, joyful poems on "an apple on the porch rail or a cat putting his foot into the jam pot" required, Shapiro felt, "a sense of propriety": "Williams was owner, and the young poet could never own Baltimore." Baltimore was owned by others — the rich old Catholic families and "the richer blue-eyed Protestants" and even the Sephardic and Germanic Jews. An offspring of Russian Jews living "on a modest car-lined street where the almost-rich Jews lived" would have to settle for being "a spy or at least a watcher."

Williams, with his direct embrace of American facts, gave Shapiro his attitude. Auden gave him his voice, "the natural modern diction and the use of words that had never appeared in poetry, textbook words, newspaper words, the convoluted syntax, the mixture of economics and love, the brilliance and the gloom." Baltimore, especially Jewish Baltimore, was a center of Communist activity; Shapiro discovered Auden in a British magazine in a Communist bookstore, and was inspired by the "long Auden historical-prophetic sweep" to write the most ambitious of his juvenile poems, a tortuous meditation on Marxism called "Irenicon," clotted with words like "trepid," "connate," and "guerdon." It is rough chewing, but at least Shapiro had taken a bite of the real city around him:

> If squirrels were rats, how ugly they would be—
> And passing the dumps, these men seem rats enough,
> In fire-silt trudging the bitterness of trash . . .

A frequent streetcar ride carried the poet past an extensive cemetery, and, as he relates in *The Younger Son*,

> he began to think of a poem about this great city of the dead, which when he wrote it would have a slightly Marxist tone of indignation, touching on the class distinctions of the cemetery world . . . It would be his first authentic poem, as he thought of it in afteryears, and for the poetics he could thank Auden, at least for the diction of the epithets.

The poem was "Necropolis," and this selection begins with it. "Necropolis," together with "University," "Midnight Show," and "Love Poem," made up the first batch of his poems accepted by *Poetry*, in August of 1940; he tells of how he read the blue note of acceptance at the trolley stop, waved the trolley past, ran back to his apartment, phoned to inform his employer (Sears Roebuck) he would not be in that day, and "sat back and read holes in the blue notice." "Auto Wreck" is another early poem whose inspiration his memoir recalls. After an evening of lovemaking with a perfume salesgirl whose sexuality receives his memoir's highest rating, he encountered, while walking the three miles back home through the summer night, a spectacular, sickening auto wreck. For more than a page he dwells upon the prosody of the poem, its iambs and spondees, and Donne's and Herbert's and Milton's bold metrics, and then explains:

> To leave her in the peace of the night and walk home in sleeping streets among sleepers, straight into this nightmare, was like the world just now, seemingly quietly going about its business but walking straight into the nightmare that nobody could stop.

The future soldier-poet was already moving toward the coming nightmare, "for the world was now wound to the utmost tightness in spite of the last détente." His anticipatory mood reached a climax in the surreal, jangling "Scyros," which was also influenced by seventeenth-century diction, its stanza based on that of Milton's "Nativity Ode." It is a poem Shapiro included in all his self-anthologies, though it is untypical—Auden at his most unconscionably jaunty—and not easy to make sense of, even when we know that Scyros is where Rupert Brooke died and that the odd epigraph "snuffle and sniff and handker-chief" is from a poem by him. Some other poems, too, are clarified by what Shapiro remembers about them. The snide tone of "University" derived from a snub delivered to him on the campus of the University of Virginia ("un-equals blankly pass"), not by a Gentile but by two German Jews who had been friendly acquaintances in Baltimore. Shapiro's mother came from Virginia, his family lived there for a time, and he thought of himself as something of a Southerner; Emporia was the Virginia town where his maternal grandfather had a dry-goods store, a modest "Emporium." On the troopship slowly taking him to Australia Shapiro used some of his time in a painstaking translation of Baudelaire's poem "Giantess." "Glass Poem" arose from a "big one-room apartment" in Aus-tralia, "full of reflections and distracting glimmers"; the poem capped his seduction of the room's inhabitant. "Phe-nomenon," he tells us in a note, "refers to the world of the Nazis," and the sonnet "Carte Postale" is easier to grasp under its final title, "French Postcard."

In general Shapiro's poems are accessible without pri-vate clues—perhaps, for New Critical tastes, too accessi-ble. Randall Jarrell, in phrasing whose subtle hostility did not prevent Shapiro from quoting it, described the poems as "fresh and young and rash and live; their hard clear out-line, their flat bold colors create a world like that of a knowing and skillful neo-primitive painting, without any of the confusion or profundity of atmosphere." Shapiro recalled of his beloved perfume salesgirl that "she was, like him, one of those born with the happiness gene," and his models, Whitman and Williams and Auden, were happy poets, busily turning the world into words. Even amid "the necessary futility of war," the poet-soldier "would not go so far as to say he was happy, but he wasn't the opposite, either; his writing saw to that." His mind-set is opposed to that of Eliot and Lowell, for whom the world is invincibly tainted, and in some distasteful way alien. Of himself Shapiro said, "To write poetry out of commonplaceness is to love or accept the common, and in fact he did." In such poems as "Auto Wreck," "Drug Store," "Buick," "Haircut," and "Honkytonk," an urban, commercialized, industrial environment is illumined and cherished in a prosody ranging from rolling, raucous anapests to packed iambic pentameter, a formal virtuosity learned from Auden and from autodidactic study of classic English poetry. The poet's tone is breezy, surly, rapturous as the mood rapidly shifts. The last lines often stub our toe and invite us to reread. The concreteness can seem defiant, in-your-face. The reader does not forget a line like the first of "The Fly": "O hideous little bat, the size of snot."

"No ideas but in things," William Carlos Williams had said. Shapiro followed the dictum but in a more ornate style than the fragmentary imagism and free-floating voices of those moderns influenced by Ezra Pound. A late poem, "Bill Williams," pays tribute to the

> Hard-working slum doc and fulltime poet
>   Whose poems were prescriptions,
> Who tried to get the monkey Ezra off his back
>   And never quite kicked the habit.

Shapiro thought a great deal about the politics of poetics and probably wrote more poems about other poets, living and dead, than any other poet of his stature. His book-length *Essay on Rime* is an earnest, methodical tour de force, an extended schoolbook exercise represented herein with a few excerpts, if only to illustrate the severe seriousness with which poetry was taken by the generation of which this one member, without research materials but as company clerk in control of a typewriter, pounded out this *summa poetica* thirty lines a day in the heat of embattled New Guinea.

The poems of *V-Letter* are somewhat looser than those of *Person, Place and Thing*, and less studious in avoiding clichés. Shapiro's tenderness and candor make them the foremost verse monument to that war's daily reality. This was American soldiering, from the receipt of V-mail on the first page ("Aside") to the sending of it on the last. In between, there was the fear of bombs falling under a full moon, an amputation, camp movies, a self-inflicted death whose commemoration accepts the perhaps inevitable rhyming of "in pain" with "not died in vain." His introduction stated, "I try to write freely, one day as a Christian, the next as a Jew, the next as a soldier who sees the gigantic slapstick of modern war." Shapiro knew he was fortunate that the army cast him—on no more basis, his memoir speculates, than his coming from the hospital town of Baltimore—as a healer rather than a killer; he wondered how well he would have done as an infantryman. As a medical corpsman, he won four bronze stars, achieved the rank of sergeant, survived air raids and landings under bombardment, witnessed much suffering, and did an impressive amount of writing and tomcatting.

His poems do not wave the flag, nor do they mock it. Like most young males of the time, he accepted the call to arms meekly: "the poet, for all his elbow-rubbing with Socialists, Communists, Trotskyites, believed in—Virginia." He recalled with distaste the phony medical discharge that a fellow-student from Baltimore arranged for himself. Some stress overseas seems indicated by his flirtation, in New Guinea, with conversion to Catholicism; an attractive fellow-student at the Pratt Library School had urged her religion on him but the chaplain brushed him off.

Traces of this Christian by-blow remain in his poems ("The Convert," "The Missal," number X of "Recapitulations," the last of "Six Religious Lyrics"). His lower-case catholicity goes with his wish to contain, like Whitman, contradictions, to cover all bets—an anti-Communist who consorts with Communists, an atheist who says his prayers. Like Bellow and Mailer, he is interested in his Jewishness, and does not disown it, but is more interested in the general enterprise of being American.

From the 1942 Australian volume *The Place of Love*, the impetuous and disheveled issue of a love affair, I have taken a brief prose poem, "My Hair," which Shapiro never reprinted, as well as the sonnet "The Tongue"; both these small poems give us a tactile intimacy not always allowed by the young poet's grave and pugnacious artifice. A selection from Shapiro's full poetic output should include enough of the early poems that established his reputation, without stinting the venturesome, often rakish later work. His first truly post-war collection was *Trial of a Poet* (1947), and I have chosen forty lines from the long title poem to illustrate his magnanimous attempt to dramatize and understand the foremost literary scandal of the decade, Ezra Pound's trial for treason and the Solomonic decision to confine him not as a traitor but as a madman. The Pound drama involved Shapiro personally, since, after being initially seduced by Eliot's personal appeal, he ended up opposing the 1948 Bollingen Prize to Pound, in which he, as the Library of Congress's former Consultant in Poetry, had a vote. Pound won anyway, but his strident anti-Semitism did not pass without editorial protest: in an article in the *Saturday Review of Literature*, Shapiro wrote, "I voted against Pound in the belief that the poet's political and moral philosophy ultimately vitiates his poetry." Characteristically, a few years later, in *Poetry*, he repeated this assertion but added, "Otherwise I can only say that the book the *Pisan Cantos* was the best book of verse of that year, and of many years."

Most of the poems in the collection *Poems of a Jew* (1958) had been published in earlier books; the volume served as a pledge of allegiance to his Jewishness, complex and elusive yet insistent as it was:

> The Jewish question, whatever that might be, is not my concern. Nor is Judaism. Nor is Jewry. Nor is Israel . . . I am one of those who views with disgust and disappointment . . . the backsliding of artists and intellectuals toward religion. . . . These poems, in any case, are not religious poems but the poems of a Jew. No one has been able to define Jew, and in essence this defiance of definition is the central meaning of Jewish consciousness. . . . As a third-generation American I grew up with the obsessive idea of personal liberty which engrosses all Americans except the oldest and richest families. As a Jew I grew up in an atmosphere of mysterious pride and sensitivity, an atmosphere in which even the greatest achievement was touched by a sense of the comic.

In spite of himself Shapiro was a ground-breaker, in a country whose literature had been predominantly Protestant since the Puritans. The only American-Jewish poet he had read as a young man was the pseudo-Biblical, now forgotten James Oppenheimer. In academic English departments, there were Lionel Trilling at Columbia and Harry Levin at Harvard and precious few others. As Shapiro wrote to Lee Bartlett, his bibliographer, "I was the second Jew to be hired at Johns Hopkins, and a good friend of mine was the first Jew to get a Ph.D. at Hopkins. This is recent history! But now of course the Jews practically run the place." He once thought of changing his name to the Waspish Karl Camden, but settled for Karl, a more Germanic, and hence higher-class, spelling than the original Carl. Even without formal Jewish affiliations, he responded to the founding of Israel with the stirring "Israel," read at a mass meeting in Baltimore, and composed long poems on Adam and Eve, David and Bathsheba, and Moses.

The title of *The Bourgeois Poet* (1964) came from the mouth of another poet, Shapiro informed his assiduous bibliographer, Lee Bartlett. After a reading in Seattle, the drunken Theodore Roethke greeted his entry at a party with, "Well, here comes the bourgeois poet!" Thence Shapiro resolved, "I was going to accept the fact that I am a bourgeois poet. . . . I wanted to say, 'Yeah, I do like living in split-level houses, and so on.'" It seems odd that Shapiro would thus be singled out, since post-war academic appointments for poets and "creative" writers had generated a large tribe of housebroken penmen and, later, penwomen, habituated to steady wages, the adoration of students, and residence in green and pleasant college communities. Nevertheless, he did feel a difficulty in "being a poet and a bourgeois American at the same time," and his upbringing among the Marxists of Baltimore perhaps lent a special sting to the epithet. The original text of the book was much longer and was edited down by the poet and his long-time editor, Albert Erskine, but, he confided to Bartlett, "I've always felt I should have re-edited it, making it less jerky and less obscure."

The published version consisted of ninety-six untitled pieces of prose ranging in length from six lines to ten pages. When some of these took their place in his *Selected Poems* (1968), they were titled with their opening words, but in *Collected Poems 1940–1978*, they were given short titles, which I have adopted here. One poem not in the 1978 volume I have titled myself ("War Movies"). That Shapiro had a taste for writing prose is evident in his numerous reviews, his several books of essays,* his two volumes of autobiography,† his messy and scabrous but animated lone novel, *Edsel*, and in his prose poems, which he produced early, after the examples of Baudelaire, Rimbaud, and Eliot. During his Library of Congress appointment he showed a copy of *The Place of Love* to the French Nobel Laureate St. John Perse, who "said that I should write in the style of 'The Dirty Word'; in other words, the prose poem."

White-Haired Lover (1968), a courtly volume of dainty slenderness, composed of sanserif apostrophes, mostly sonnets, to his second wife; *Adult Bookstore* (1976), whose venues have moved from Nebraska and Chicago to California, and whose title was also that of a movie he made but that was "too hot" to distribute; *The Old Horsefly* (1992), dedicated to his third wife in the Latin of Horace and crotchety-magisterial in tone: these volumes returned the bourgeois prose-poet to the conventional look of verse on the page.

* *Beyond Criticism* (1953); *In Defense of Ignorance* (1960); *To Abolish Children and Other Essays* (1968); *The Poetry Wreck: Selected Essays 1950–1970* (1975).

† The second volume, *Reports of My Death*, came out in 1990, two years after *The Younger Son*. It is relatively diffuse and dispirited as it sketches the literary and academic life experienced after 1945 by the returned soldier-poet. In the first volume, poetry is his *princesse lointaine*; in the second, he has married her. His offhand, rather truculent prose picks up in the last two chapters. The depression and attempted suicide of his second wife weirdly metamorphose into false journalistic reports of his own suicide, which depress him. Teri's swift death by cancer is soon followed by the advent of Shapiro's third wife, Sophie; the last chapter describes a visit he and she, a native Austrian, paid to the tomb of his hero, Auden, and the poem that resulted.

There is little trace of Auden's metrical acrobatics and deft hand with great issues, though the presumptions of the militant radicals do lead Shapiro to compose a sestina parodying the vocabulary of the counter-culture militants. He became conservative, or perhaps had always been, growing up skeptical among Baltimore's Communists. He writes in *The Old Horsefly* of what has always concerned him most, poetry and poets—Whitman and Williams, Ovid and Hopkins, Joyce and Stevens, and Eliot and Pound, who functioned not only as his *bêtes noires* but his *points de départ*, the inescapable modernists. With his untiring eye for American facts he writes about Kleenex, New York City, the plague of Creative Writing, "stronger than gonorrhea," and "Fucking," of which he disingenuously confesses, "I never got the hang of it, really."

In his lifetime Shapiro published, aside from *Poems of a Jew*, five selections of his own work: *Poems 1940–1953, Selected Poems* (1968), *Collected Poems 1940–1978, Love and War, Art and God: The Poems of Karl Shapiro* (1984), and *New & Selected Poems 1940–1986* (1987). This last distillation is just over a hundred pages long; any poem in it shunned in my own selection I reread attentively, hoping to like it better. I have partaken sparingly of Shapiro the balladeer and deviser of historical tableaux — Beethoven dying, Commodore Perry seeking admission to Japan. He has a mood of lofty apostrophe which can become overbearing, and which makes his smaller, airier lyrics appealing to an anthologist. My choices are arranged in roughly chronological order, in line with known magazine publication dates, his own accountings, and the move into wartime and back. I have kept, after omitting about half, the poems from *V-Letter* in the sequence devised by his loving agent.

When a poet makes a selection of himself, there are elements of suppression, of reshaping his work in line with the ongoing creativity. Perspectives change again with an artist's death. He becomes an inhabitant of history, an index to certain global moments. And we treasure, more than he did, revelations of the man, the personality, with his soft spots for war and Christmas and tough plebeian streets, his habits of contention and sentiment, his "American slouch," as he wrote in *The Younger Son*:

> The poet must wear his uniform lightly, and unlike the General's it is not part of his skin ... He must wear his America lightly like a civilian, he must glow with it and not flaunt it. It was part of his luck, his ease, part of the American slouch.

He aimed to be what the Germans called a *Dinge Dichter*, a *thing* poet. "The substantive [*Person, Place and Thing*; *Noun*] fascinated him, as something to fix upon, and hold on to." His feet planted on the substantive, he could be modest and casual but also bold, with the boldness of truth personally verified. Though best remembered, still, as the poet in khaki, Shapiro's long peacetime life was devoted to the modernist battle, a fight for the specific and honestly felt, a rescue of language from poetic conventions, easy assumptions, usages worn smooth, polite palaver, rhetoric:

> That was the enemy, rhetoric, and always had been. Leave patriotic and antipatriotic to John Philip Sousa. Poets had tastier fish to fry—what soldiering was like, what it did to the man, the soul, the poetry, and the artifacts everywhere, the Buicks, the university, the grandmothers, the flies, oh the flies, American flies in Petersburg, Virginia.

John Updike
2002

Necropolis

Even in death they prosper; even in the death
Where lust lies senseless and pride fallow
The mouldering owners of rents and labor
Prosper and improve the high hill.

For theirs is the stone whose name is deepest cut,
Theirs the facsimile temple, theirs
The iron acanthus and the hackneyed Latin,
The boxwood rows and all the birds.

And even in death the poor are thickly herded
In intimate congestion under streets and alleys.
Look at the standard sculpture, the cheap
Synonymous slabs, the machined crosses.

Yes, even in death the cities are unplanned.
The heirs govern from the old centers;
They will not remove. And the ludicrous angels,
Remains of the poor, will never fly
But only multiply in the green grass.

Auto Wreck

Its quick soft silver bell beating, beating,
And down the dark one ruby flare
Pulsing out red light like an artery,
The ambulance at top speed floating down
Past beacons and illuminated clocks
Wings in a heavy curve, dips down,
And brakes speed, entering the crowd.
The doors leap open, emptying light;
Stretchers are laid out, the mangled lifted
And stowed into the little hospital.
Then the bell, breaking the hush, tolls once,
And the ambulance with its terrible cargo
Rocking, slightly rocking, moves away,
As the doors, an afterthought, are closed.

We are deranged, walking among the cops
Who sweep glass and are large and composed.
One is still making notes under the light.
One with a bucket douches ponds of blood
Into the street and gutter.
One hangs lanterns on the wrecks that cling,
Empty husks of locusts, to iron poles.

Our throats were tight as tourniquets,
Our feet were bound with splints, but now,
Like convalescents intimate and gauche,
We speak through sickly smiles and warn
With the stubborn saw of common sense,
The grim joke and the banal resolution.

The traffic moves around with care,
But we remain, touching a wound
That opens to our richest horror.
Already old, the question Who shall die?
Becomes unspoken Who is innocent?

For death in war is done by hands;
Suicide has cause and stillbirth, logic;
And cancer, simple as a flower, blooms.
But this invites the occult mind,
Cancels our physics with a sneer,
And spatters all we knew of denouement
Across the expedient and wicked stones.

The Dome of Sunday

With focus sharp as Flemish-painted face
In film of varnish brightly fixed
And through a polished hand-lens deeply seen,
Sunday at noon through hyaline thin air
Sees down the street,
And in the camera of my eye depicts
Row-houses and row-lives:
Glass after glass, door after door the same,
Face after face the same, the same,
The brutal visibility the same;

As if one life emerging from one house
Would pause, a single image caught between
Two facing mirrors where vision multiplies

Beyond perspective,
A silent clatter in the high-speed eye
Spinning out photo-circulars of sight.

I see slip to the curb the long machines
Out of whose warm and windowed rooms pirouette
Shellacked with silk and light
The hard legs of our women.
Our women are one woman, dressed in black.
The carmine printed mouth
And cheeks as soft as muslin-glass belong
Outright to one dark dressy man,
Merely a swagger at her curvy side.
This is their visit to themselves:
All day from porch to porch they weave
A nonsense pattern through the even glare,
Stealing in surfaces
Cold vulgar glances at themselves.

And high up in the heated room all day
I wait behind the plate glass pane for one,
Hot as a voyeur for a glimpse of one,
The vision to blot out this woman's sheen;
All day my sight records expensively
Row-houses and row-lives.

But nothing happens; no diagonal
With melting shadow falls across the curb:
Neither the blinded negress lurching through fatigue,
Nor exiles bleeding from their pores,
Nor that bright bomb slipped lightly from its rack
To splinter every silvered glass and crystal prism,

Witch-bowl and perfume bottle
And billion candle-power dressing-bulb,
No direct hit to smash the shatter-proof
And lodge at last the quivering needle
Clean in the eye of one who stands transfixed
In fascination of her brightness.

Epitaph for John and Richard

There goes the clock; there goes the sun;
Greenwich is right with Arlington;
The signal's minutes are signifying
That somebody old has finished dying,
That somebody young has just begun.

What do you think you earned today
Except the waste, except the pay,
Except the power to be spending?
And now your year is striking, ending,
What do you think you have put away?

Only a promise, only a life
Squandered in secret with a wife
In bedtime feigning and unfeigning;
The blood has long since ceased complaining;
The clock has satisfied the strife.

They will not cast your honored head
Or say from lecterns what you said,
But only keep you with them all
Committed in the City Hall;
Once born, once married, and once dead.

Drug Store

I do remember an apothecary,
And hereabouts 'a dwells

It baffles the foreigner like an idiom,
And he is right to adopt it as a form
Less serious than the living-room or bar;
        For it disestablishes the café,
Is a collective, and on basic country.

Not that it praises hygiene and corrupts
The ice-cream parlor and the tobacconist's
Is it a center; but that the attractive symbols
        Watch over puberty and leer
Like rubber bottles waiting for sick-use.

Youth comes to jingle nickels and crack wise;
The baseball scores are his, the magazines
Devoted to lust, the jazz, the Coca-Cola,
        The lending-library of love's latest.
He is the customer; he is heroized.

And every nook and cranny of the flesh
Is spoken to by packages with wiles.
"Buy me, buy me," they whimper and cajole;
        The hectic range of lipsticks pouts,
Revealing the wicked and the simple mouth.

With scarcely any evasion in their eye
They smoke, undress their girls, exact a stance;
But only for a moment. The clock goes round;
        Crude fellowships are made and lost;
They slump in booths like rags, not even drunk.

Haircut

O wonderful nonsense of lotions of Lucky Tiger,
Of savory soaps and oils of bottle-bright green,
The gold of liqueurs, the unguents of Newark and
      Niger,
Powders and balms and waters washing me clean;

In mirrors of marble and silver I see us forever
Increasing, decreasing the puzzles of luminous spaces
As I turn, am revolved and am pumped in the air on a
      lever,
With the backs of my heads in chorus with all of my
      faces.

Scissors and comb are mowing my hair into neatness,
Now pruning my ears, now smoothing my neck like a
      plain;
In the harvest of hair and the chaff of powdery sweetness
My snow-covered slopes grow dark with the wooly
      rain.

And the little boy cries, for it hurts to sever the curl,
And we too are quietly bleating to part with our coat.
Does the barber want blood in a dish? I am weak as a girl,
I desire my pendants, the fatherly chin of a goat.

I desire the pants of a bear, the nap of a monkey
Which trousers of friction have blighted down to my
      skin.
I am bare as a tusk, as jacketed up as a flunkey,
With the chest of a moth-eaten camel growing within.

But in death we shall flourish, you summer-dark leaves
    of my head,
While the flesh of the jaw ebbs away from the shores of
    my teeth;
You shall cover my sockets and soften the boards of my
    bed
And lie on the flat of my temples as proud as a wreath.

Mongolian Idiot

A dog that spoke, a monster born of sheep
We mercilessly kill, and kill the thought,
Yet house the parrot and let the centaur go,
These being to their nature and those not.
We laugh at apes, that never quite succeed
        At eating soup or wearing hats.

Adam had named so many but not this,
This that would name a curse when it had come,
Unfinished man, or witch, or myth, or sin,
Not ever father and never quite a son.
Ape had outstripped him, dog and darling lamb
        And all the kindergarten beasts.

Enter the bare room of his mind and count
His store of words with letters large and black;
See how he handles clumsily those blocks
With swans and sums; his colored picture books.
At thirty-five he squeals to see the ball
        Bounce in the air and roll away.

Pity and fear we give this innocent
Who maimed his mother's beautiful instinct;
But she would say, "My body had a dog;
I bore the ape and nursed the crying sheep.
He is my kindness and my splendid gift
          Come from all life and for all life."

Scyros

snuffle and sniff and handkerchief

   The doctor punched my vein
   The captain called me Cain
Upon my belly sat the sow of fear
   With coins on either eye
   The President came by
And whispered to the braid what none could hear

   High over where the storm
   Stood steadfast cruciform
The golden eagle sank in wounded wheels
   White Negroes laughing still
   Crept fiercely on Brazil
Turning the navies upward on their keels

   Now one by one the trees
   Stripped to their naked knees
To dance upon the heaps of shrunken dead
   The roof of England fell
   Great Paris tolled her bell
And China staunched her milk and wept for bread

No island singly lay
But lost its name that day
The Ainu dived across the plunging sands
From dawn to dawn to dawn
King George's birds came on
Strafing the tulips from his children's hands

Thus in the classic sea
Southeast from Thessaly
The dynamited mermen washed ashore
And tritons dressed in steel
Trolled heads with rod and reel
And dredged potatoes from the Aegean floor

Hot is the sky and green
Where Germans have been seen
The moon leaks metal on the Atlantic fields
Pink boys in birthday shrouds
Loop lightly through the clouds
Or coast the peaks of Finland on their shields

That prophet year by year
Lay still but could not hear
Where scholars tapped to find his new remains
Gog and Magog ate pork
In vertical New York
And war began next Wednesday on the Danes.

Elegy for Two Banjos

Haul up the flag, you mourners,
        Not half-mast but all the way;
The funeral is done and disbanded;
        The devil's had the final say.

O mistress and wife too pensive,
        Pallbearers and priestly men,
Put your black clothes in the attic,
        And get up on your feet again.

Death did his job like a scholar,
        A most unusual case,
Death did his job like a gentleman;
        He barely disturbed the face.

You packed him in a handsome carton,
        Set the lid with silver screws;
You dug a dark pit in the graveyard
        To tell the white worms the news.

Now you've nothing left to remember,
        Nothing but the words he wrote,
But they'll never let you remember,
        Only stick like a bone in your throat.

O if I'd been his wife or mistress,
        His pallbearer or his parish priest,
I'd have kept him at home forever—
        Or as long as bric-a-brac at least.

I would have burned his body
        And salvaged a sizeable bone
For a paper-weight or a door-stop
        Or a garden flagstone.

I would have heaped the fire
        And boiled his beautiful skull.
It was laden like a ship for travels
        And now is but an empty hull.

I would have dried it off in linens,
        Polished it with a chamois cloth
Till it shone like a brand-new quarter
        And felt smooth as the nose of a moth.

Or I'd have hung it out in the garden
        Where everything else is alive,
Put a queen bee in the brain case
        So the bees could build a hive.

Maybe I'd have wired the jawbone
        With a silver spring beneath,
Set it in the cradle with baby
        So baby could rattle the teeth.

O you didn't do right by William
        To shove him down that filthy hole,
Throw him a lot of tears and Latin
        And a cheap "God bless your soul."

You might as well leave off mourning,
        His photograph is getting dim,

So you'd better take a long look at it
    For it's all you'll ever see of him.

Haul up the flag, you mourners,
    Not half-mast but all the way;
The funeral is done and disbanded;
    The devil's had the final say.

Buick

As a sloop with a sweep of immaculate wing on her
    delicate spine
And a keel as steel as a root that holds in the sea as she
    leans,
Leaning and laughing, my warm-hearted beauty, you
    ride, you ride,
You tack on the curves with parabola speed and a kiss of
    goodbye,
Like a thoroughbred sloop, my new high-spirited spirit,
    my kiss.

As my foot suggests that you leap in the air with your
    hips of a girl,
My finger that praises your wheel and announces your
    voices of song,
Flouncing your skirts, you blueness of joy, you flirt of
    politeness,
You leap, you intelligence, essence of wheelness with
    silvery nose,
And your platinum clocks of excitement stir like the
    hairs of a fern.

But how alien you are from the booming belts of your
 birth and the smoke
Where you turned on the stinging lathes of Detroit and
 Lansing at night
And shrieked at the torch in your secret parts and the
 amorous tests,
But now with your eyes that enter the future of roads
 you forget;
You are all instinct with your phosphorous glow and
 your streaking hair.

And now when we stop it is not as the bird from the
 shell that I leave
Or the leathery pilot who steps from his bird with a
 sneer of delight,
And not as the ignorant beast do you squat and watch
 me depart,
But with exquisite breathing you smile, with satisfaction
 of love,
And I touch you again as you tick in the silence and
 settle in sleep.

The Fly

O hideous little bat, the size of snot,
With polyhedral eye and shabby clothes,
To populate the stinking cat you walk
The promontory of the dead man's nose,
Climb with the fine leg of a Duncan-Phyfe

The smoking mountains of my food
   And in a comic mood
In mid-air take to bed a wife.

Riding and riding with your filth of hair
On gluey foot or wing, forever coy,
Hot from the compost and green sweet decay,
Sounding your buzzer like an urchin toy—
You dot all whiteness with diminutive stool,
   In the tight belly of the dead
      Burrow with hungry head
   And inlay maggots like a jewel.

At your approach the great horse stomps and paws
Bringing the hurricane of his heavy tail;
Shod in disease you dare to kiss my hand
Which sweeps against you like an angry flail;
Still you return, return, trusting your wing
   To draw you from the hunter's reach
      That learns to kill to teach
   Disorder to the tinier thing.

My peace is your disaster. For your death
Children like spiders cup their pretty hands
And wives resort to chemistry of war.
In fens of sticky paper and quicksands
You glue yourself to death. Where you are stuck
   You struggle hideously and beg,
      You amputate your leg
   Imbedded in the amber muck.

But I, a man, must swat you with my hate,
Slap you across the air and crush your flight,
Must mangle with my shoe and smear your blood,
Expose your little guts pasty and white,
Knock your head sidewise like a drunkard's hat,
   Pin your wings under like a crow's,
     Tear off your flimsy clothes
   And beat you as one beats a rat.

Then like Gargantua I stride among
The corpses strewn like raisins in the dust,
The broken bodies of the narrow dead
That catch the throat with fingers of disgust.
I sweep. One gyrates like a top and falls
   And stunned, stone blind, and deaf
     Buzzes its frightful F
   And dies between three cannibals.

The Snob

At what time in its little history
Did on the matrix of his brain a blow
Fall that struck like a relentless die
And left him speechless; or was it by degrees
That the algid folds of mind, caught in a pose,
                 Hardened and set like concrete,
Printing and fixing a distorted moment?

Nothing but death will smash this ugly cast
That wears its trade mark big upon its face,

A scutcheon for Greek-letter brotherhoods
Where it is weakly sworn by smiles to cow
Unequals, niggers or just Methodists.
                    His bearing is a school of thought,
But he is not funny and not unimportant.

University

To hurt the Negro and avoid the Jew
Is the curriculum. In mid-September
The entering boys, identified by hats,
Wander in a maze of mannered brick
        Where boxwood and magnolia brood
        And columns with imperious stance
        Like rows of ante-bellum girls
            Eye them, outlanders.

In whited cells, on lawns equipped for peace,
Under the arch, and lofty banister,
Equals shake hands, unequals blankly pass;
The exemplary weather whispers, "Quiet, quiet"
        And visitors on tiptoe leave
        For the raw North, the unfinished West,
        As the young, detecting an advantage,
            Practice a face.

Where, on their separate hill, the colleges,
Like manor houses of an older law,
Gaze down embankments on a land in fee,
The Deans, dry spinsters over family plate,

Ring out the English name like coin,
Humor the snob and lure the lout.
Within the precincts of this world
   Poise is a club.

But on the neighboring range, misty and high,
The past is absolute: some luckless race
Dull with inbreeding and conformity
Wears out its heart, and comes barefoot and bad
   For charity or jail. The scholar
   Sanctions their obsolete disease;
   The gentleman revolts with shame
      At his ancestor.

And the true nobleman, once a democrat,
Sleeps on his private mountain. He was one
Whose thought was shapely and whose dream was broad;
This school he held his art and epitaph.
   But now it takes from him his name,
   Falls open like a dishonest look,
   And shows us, rotted and endowed,
      Its senile pleasure.

Washington Cathedral

   From summer and the wheel-shaped city
   That sweats like a swamp and wrangles on
   Its melting streets, white mammoth Forums,
And political hotels with awnings, caryatids;

Past barricaded embassies with trees
    That shed trash and parch his eyes,
To here, the acres of superior quiet,
    Shadow and damp, the tourist comes,
    And, cooled by stones and darkness, stares.

    Tall as a lover's night, the nave
    Broods over him, irradiates,
And stars of color out of painted glass
Shoot downward on apostles and on chairs
Huddled by hundreds under altar rails.
Yet it is only Thursday; there are no prayers,

But exclamations. The lady invokes by name
    The thousand-odd small sculptures, spooks,
    New angels, pitted roods; she gives
The inventory of relics to his heart
That aches with history and astonishment:
He gives a large coin to a wooden coffer.

Outside, noon blazes in his face like guns.
He goes down by the Bishop's walk, the dial,
    The expensive grass, the Byzantine bench,
While stark behind him a red naked crane
    Hangs over the unfinished transept,
A Cubist hen rivalling the Gothic School.

Whether he sees the joke; whether he cares;
Whether he tempts a vulgar miracle,
Some deus ex machina, this is his choice,

A shrine of whispers and tricky penumbras.
    Therefore he votes again for the paid
Clergy, the English hint, the bones of Wilson
Crushed under tons of fake magnificence.
    Nor from the zoo of his instincts
    Come better than crude eagles: now
He cannot doubt that violent obelisk
And Lincoln whittled to a fool's colossus.
This church and city triumph in his eyes.
He is only a good alien, nominally happy.

Emporium

    He must have read Aladdin who rubbed his head
    And brought this out of space; some genie came
    With bolts of lawn and rugs of heavy red,
    Shoes for white boxes, gems for velvet trays;
    For who could authorize in his right name
Such pricelessness of time and recklessness of days?

    Not Faust, who longed for Hell, would sell his light
    For moving stairs and mirrors set in miles
    Where wives might wander with their sex in sight;
    Rage and rat's-logic this man must have known
    Who built these buttresses on rotted piles,
Initialed every brick, and carved his lips in stone.

    As if the ancient principle obtained
    And solvent time would underwrite his debt,
    Or the strong face of flesh were not profaned
    For mannikins with hair of cloth-of-gold;

As if no tongue had ever questioned yet
Who buys and who is bought, who sells and who is sold.

    But those politely dressed in normal drab
    Shall think of him remotely, think with shame
    How of their skill, their goodness and their gab
    He trained his joys to be obsequious Jews;
    At last not even wives shall goad his name
To feats of wealth, humility, and sickness-news;

So that, with rounded ruins honored, like Stonehenge,
Time shall have time, and he his impotent revenge.

My Grandmother

My grandmother moves to my mind in context of
    sorrow
And, as if apprehensive of near death, in black;
Whether erect in chair, her dry and corded throat
    harangued by grief,
Or at ragged book bent in Hebrew prayer,
Or gentle, submissive, and in tears to strangers;
Whether in sunny parlor or back of drawn blinds.

Though time and tongue made any love disparate,
On daguerreotype with classic perspective
Beauty I sigh and soften at is hers.
I pity her life of deaths, the agony of her own,
But most that history moved her through
Stranger lands and many houses,
Taking her exile for granted, confusing
The tongues and tasks of her children's children.

October 1

That season when the leaf deserts the bole
And half-dead see-saws through the October air
Falling face-downward on the walks to print
The decalcomania of its little soul—
Hardly has the milkman's sleepy horse
On wooden shoes echoed across the blocks,
When with its back jaws open like a dredge
The van comes lumbering up the curb to someone's
    door and knocks.

And four black genii muscular and shy
Holding their shy caps enter the first room
Where someone hurriedly surrenders up
The thickset chair, the mirror half awry,
Then to their burdens stoop without a sound.
One with his bare hands rends apart the bed,
One stuffs the china-barrel with stale print,
Two bear the sofa toward the door with dark funereal
    tread.

The corner lamp, the safety eye of night,
Enveloped in the sun blinks and goes blind
And soon the early risers pick their way
Through kitchenware and pillows bolt upright.
The bureau on the sidewalk with bare back
And wrinkling veneer is most disgraced,
The sketch of Paris suffers in the wind,
Only the bike, its nose against the wall, does not show
    haste.

Two hours—the movers mop their necks and look,
Filing through dust and echoes back and forth.
The halls are hollow and all the floors are cleared
Bare to the last board, to the most secret nook;
But on the street a small chaos survives
That slowly now the leviathan ingests,
And schoolboys and stenographers stare at
The truck, the house, the husband in his hat who stands
    and rests.

He turns with miserable expectant face
And for the last time enters. On the wall
A picture-stain spreads from the nail-hole down.
Each object live and dead has left its trace.
He leaves his key; but as he quickly goes
This question comes behind: Did someone die?
Is someone rich or poor, better or worse?
What shall uproot a house and bring this care into his
    eye?

The Confirmation

When mothers weep and fathers richly proud
Worship on Sunday morning their tall son
And girls in white like angels in a play
    Tiptoe between the potted palms
    And all the crimson windows pray,
        The preacher bound in black
Opens his hands like pages of a book
    And holds the black and crimson law
    For every boy to look.

Last night between the chapters of a dream,
The photograph still sinning in the drawer,
The boy awoke; the moon shone in the yard
    On hairy hollyhocks erect
    And buds of roses pink and hard
        And on the solid wall
A square of light like movies fell to pose
    An actress naked in the night
        As hollyhock and rose.

And to confirm his sex, breathless and white
With benediction self-bestowed he knelt
Oh tightly married to his childish grip,
    And unction smooth as holy-oil
    Fell from the vessel's level lip
        Upon the altar-cloth;
Like Easter boys the blood sang in his head
    And all night long the tallow beads
        Like tears dried in the bed.

Come from the church, you parents and you girls,
And walk with kisses and with happy jokes
Beside this man. Be doubly proud, you priest,
    Once for his passion in the rose,
    Once for his body self-released;
        And speak aloud of her
Who in the perfect consciousness of joy
    Stood naked in the electric light
    And woke the hidden boy.

Honkytonk

Taken as diagram of Mind that marks,
Led by an arrow, green perimeters
Where thoughts sip peace and garden; inward then
To suffering junctions, slums kicked by a boot,
       Arpeggios of porches:
       Decision, Anger, Pride,
Like Self-Reproach the city points to this
Its maudlin slapping heart, our origin.

Then at the outskirts of our Conscious, No
From old high-over offices beats down
On standard faces Business-mad, and girls,
Grass under sullen stone, grown pale with work;
       Yet shields with shadow this
       Disgraced like genitals
Ghetto of local sin, laughable Hell,
Night's very alley, loathed but let alone.

I say to harass projects of decorum
This is maintained by kids, police, douceurs,
And ravenous for marvels, rancid Jews.
Callow as brass, their eyes on nipples snagged,
       Snagged in the jaded hair,
       Goaded by silken legs,
They mill around, bacterial and bright,
Seeking outbreaks of pain, their bitter milk.

Who needs Revenge or Fear can buy: in bars
Murals of lust, and talk; movies for men;
A waxworks of syphilitics; shooting range,
Phrenologist and tattoo artist; all
          Quacks who apprehend
          And speak the dirty word.
But oh, ridiculously lost those four
Hymning salvation at the Burlesk door.

How elemental ions of pure joy
Convert to deadly sins, and bump like trucks
Uptown to roads instinctive to the young,
I only ask. But in and out they go
          Satanic to discover
          Imago of Unrest
Whose Ultima Thule is a general low
And obscene civics of our self-distrust.

Hollywood

Farthest from any war, unique in time
Like Athens or Baghdad, this city lies
Between dry purple mountains and the sea.
The air is clear and famous, every day
Bright as a postcard, bringing bungalows
   And sights. The broad nights advertise
For love and music and astronomy.

Heart of a continent, the hearts converge
On open boulevards where palms are nursed
With flare-pots like a grove, on villa roads
Where castles cultivated like a style
Breed fabulous metaphors in foreign stone,
    And on enormous movie lots
Where history repeats its vivid blunders.

Alice and Cinderella are most real.
Here may the tourist, quite sincere at last,
Rest from his dream of travels. All is new,
No ruins claim his awe, and permanence,
Despised like customs, fails at every turn.
    Here where the eccentric thrives,
Laughter and love are leading industries.

Luck is another. Here the bodyguard,
The parasite, the scholar are well paid,
The quack erects his alabaster office,
The moron and the genius are enshrined,
And the mystic makes a fortune quietly;
    Here all superlatives come true
And beauty is marketed like a basic food.

O can we understand it? Is it ours,
A crude whim of a beginning people,
A private orgy in a secluded spot?
Or alien like the word *harem*, or true
Like hideous Pittsburgh or depraved Atlanta?
    Is adolescence just as vile
As this its architecture and its talk?

Or are they parvenus, like boys and girls?
Or ours and happy, cleverest of all?
Yes. Yes. Though glamorous to the ignorant
This is the simplest city, a new school.
What is more nearly ours? If soul can mean
   The civilization of the brain,
This is a soul, a possible proud Florence.

The Birds

        Wrong about birds. I cannot call
        That swift, enslaved, mechanical
        Come and go, come and go,
        Build and feed and mate and grow
           Beautiful.
        Beautiful, the poets are wrong
To love you for your turn and wheel and glide and song.

        Beast of the wind, wolf of the tree,
        Heart with the gunner's history,
        Rise and fall, rise and fall,
        Heart of the heart I cannot call
           Liberty.
        Liberty, the poets are wrong
To love you for your turn and wheel and glide and song.

A Cut Flower

I stand on slenderness all fresh and fair,
I feel root-firmness in the earth far down,
I catch in the wind and loose my scent for bees
That sack my throat for kisses and suck love.
What is the wind that brings thy body over?
Wind, I am beautiful and sick. I long
For rain that strikes and bites like cold and hurts.
Be angry, rain, for dew is kind to me
When I am cool from sleep and take my bath.

Who softens the sweet earth about my feet,
Touches my face so often and brings water?
Where does she go, taller than any sunflower
Over the grass like birds? Has she a root?
These are great animals that kneel to us,
Sent by the sun perhaps to help us grow.
I have seen death. The colors went away,
The petals grasped at nothing and curled tight.
Then the whole head fell off and left the sky.

She tended me and held me by my stalk.
Yesterday I was well, and then the gleam,
The thing sharper than frost cut me in half.
I fainted and was lifted high. I feel
Waist-deep in rain. My face is dry and drawn.
My beauty leaks into the glass like rain.
When first I opened to the sun I thought
My colors would be parched. Where are my bees?
Must I die now? Is this a part of life?

Terminal

Over us stands the broad electric face
With semaphores that flick into the gaps,
Notching the time on sixtieths of space,
Springing the traveller through the folded traps
Downstairs with luggage anywhere to go
While others happily toil upward too;
Well-dressed or stricken, banished or restored,
Hundreds step down and thousands get aboard.

In neat confusion, tickets in our brain
We press the hard plush to our backs and sigh;
The brakeman thumbs his watch, the children strain
The windows to their smeary sight—Goodbye,
The great car creaks, the stone wall turns away
And lights flare past like fishes undersea;
Heads rolling heavily and all as one
With languid screams we charge into the sun.

Now through the maelstrom of the town we ride
Clicking with speed like skates on solid ice;
Streets drop and buildings silently collide,
Rails spread apart, converge and neatly splice.
Through gasping blanks of air we pound and ford
Bulking our courage forward like a road,
Climbing the world on long dead-level stairs
With catwalk stilts and trestles hung by hairs.

Out where the oaks on wide turntables grow
And constellation hamlets gyre and glow,
The straight-up bridges dive and from below

The river's sweet eccentric borders flow;
Into the culverts sliced like lands of meat,
Armies of cornstalks on their ragged feet,
And upward-outward toward the blueback hill
Where clouds of thunder graze and drink their fill.

And always at our side, swifter than we
The racing rabbits of the wire lope
And in their blood the words at liberty
Outspeed themselves; but on our rail we grope
Drinking from one white wire overhead
Hot drinks of action and hell's fiery feed.
Lightly the finger-shaped antennae feel
And lightly cheer the madness of our wheel.

We turn, we turn, thrumming the harp of sounds
And all is pleasure's move, motion of joy;
Now we imagine that we go like hounds
And now like sleds and now like many a toy
Coming alive on Christmas Day to crawl
Between the great world of the floor and wall,
But on the peak of speed we flag and fall—
Fixed on the air we do not move at all.

Arrived at space we settle in our car
And stare like souls admitted to the sky;
Nothing at length is close at hand or far;
All feats of image vanish from the eye.
Upon our brow is set the bursting star,
Upon the void the wheel and axle-bar,
The planetary fragments broken lie;
Distance is dead and light can only die.

Conscription Camp

Your landscape sickens with a dry disease
Even in May, Virginia, and your sweet pines
Like Frenchmen runted in a hundred wars
Are of a child's height in these battlefields.

For Wilson sowed his teeth where generals prayed
—High-sounding Lafayette and sick-eyed Lee—
The loud Elizabethan crashed your swamps
Like elephants and the subtle Indian fell.

Is it for love, you ancient-minded towns,
That on the tidy grass of your great graves
And on your roads and riverways serene
Between the corn with green flags in a row,

Wheat amorous as hair and hills like breasts
Each generation, ignorant of the last,
Mumbling in sheds, embarrassed to salute,
Comes back to choke on etiquette of hate?

You manufacture history like jute—
Labor is cheap, Virginia, for high deeds,
But in your British dream of reputation
The black man is your conscience and your cost.

Here on the plains perfect for civil war
The clapboard city like a weak mirage
Of order rises from the sand to house
These thousands and the paranoid Monroe;

The sunrise gun rasps in the throat of heaven;
The lungs of dawn are heavy and corrupt;
We hawk and spit; our flag walks through the air
Breathing hysteria thickly in each face.

Through the long school of day, absent in heart,
Distant in every thought but self we tread,
Wheeling in blocks like large expensive toys
That never understand except through fun.

To steal aside as aimlessly as curs
Is our desire; to stare at corporals
As sceptically as boys; not to believe
The misty-eyed letter and the cheap snapshot.

To cross the unnatural frontier of your name
Is our free dream, Virginia, and beyond,
White and unpatriotic in our beds,
To rise from sleep like driftwood out of surf.

But stricter than parole is this same wall
And these green clothes, a secret on the fields,
In towns betray us to the arresting touch
Of lady-wardens, good and evil wives.

And far and fabulous is the word "Outside"
Like "Europe" when the midnight liners sailed,
Leaving a wake of ermine on the tide
Where rubies drowned and eyes were softly drunk.

Still we abhor your news and every voice
Except the Personal Enemy's, and songs
That pumped by the great central heart of love
On tides of energy at evening come.

Instinctively to break your compact law
Box within box, Virginia, and throw down
The dangerous bright habits of pure form
We struggle hideously and cry for fear.

And like a very tired whore who stands
Wrapped in the sensual crimson of her art
High in the tired doorway of a street
And beckons half-concealed the passerby,

The sun, Virginia, on your Western stairs
Pauses and smiles away between the trees,
Motioning the soldier overhill to town
To his determined hungry burst of joy.

Giantess

When Nature once in lustful hot undress
Conceived gargantuan offspring, then would I
Have loved to live near a young giantess,
Like a voluptuous cat at a queen's feet.

To see her body flower with her desire
And freely spread out in its dreadful play,
Guess if her heart concealed some heavy fire
Whose humid smokes would swim upon her eye;

To feel at leisure her stupendous shapes,
Crawl on the cliffs of her enormous knees,
And, when the unhealthy summer suns fatigued,

Have her stretch out across the plains and so
Sleep in the shadows of her breasts at ease
Like a small hamlet at a mountain's base.

(Baudelaire translation)

My Hair

The dog's-coat of my hair is a great worry. When it is short it bristles and sparks, so that people have the temptation to approach and put their hand on it. When it is long it piles up in a solid springy wave that appears impenetrable. To brush it closes my eyes sleepily and to comb it angers me. It yields to suds and warm water but I am not beguiled—the exhaustion of hair is an old story to me! To oil it with pungent oil cleanses me throughout; I shall inhale my hat. Clip me not over the ears Jenny admired but use the scissors. The hot hot water, the cold cold water. The natural state, however, is a dry strong rug at the very extremity of my existence. The natural state is a Welcome Mat for your interested soft hand. The towel please. You were very cruel to say so.

The Tongue

As a slug on the flat of the sun-heated clay,
With the spit of its track left behind it like glass,
Imperceptibly voyages, licking its way
In the sinuous slime of itself to the grass,

So my tongue on the white-heated wall of your thigh
Licks its belly across, and the path of my slime
Lies in ribbons of passion, the wet and the dry
Overlapping to mount to the leaf of its climb.

And the mouth and the mouth and the tongue and the
    tongue
Are the fishes that feed in the joy of our oil,
And the slug of our wetness finds green food among
The hair-forests of longing where serpents uncoil.

Aside

Mail-day, and over the world in a thousand drag-nets
    The bundles of letters are dumped on the docks
        and beaches,
    And all that is dear to the personal conscious reaches
Around us again like filings around iron magnets,
And war stands aside for an hour and looks at our faces
Of total absorption that seem to have lost their places.

O demobilized for a moment, a world is made human,
    Returns to a time that is neither the present or then,
    But a garland of clippings and wishes of who-
        knows-when,
A time of its own creation, a thing of acumen
That keeps us, like movies, alive with a purpose, aside
From the play-acting truth of the newsreel in which we
        have died.

And aside from the candy and pictures and books we
        receive,
    As if we were patients whose speedy recovery were
        certain,
    There is proof of the End and the lights and the
        bow at the curtain,
After which we shall smile at each other and get up to
        leave.

Aside from the play in the play there is all that is fact,
These letters, the battle in progress, the place of the act.

And the optimal joy of the conflict, the tears of the ads
  May move us or not, and the movies at night in the
    palms
  May recall us or not to the kiss, and on Sunday the
    psalms
May remind us of Sunday or not, but aside from the lads
Who arrive like our letters still fresh from the kiss and
    the tear,
There are mouths that are dusty and eyes that are wider
    than fear.

Say no more of the dead than a prayer, say no more of
    the land
  Where the body is laid in the coral than that it is far;
  Take your finger away from the map of wherever-
    we-are,
For we lie in the map of the chart of your elderly hand;
Do not hasten the future; in agony too there is time
For the growth of the rose of the spirit astir in the slime.

For aside from ourselves as we are there is nothing alive
  Except as it keeps us alive, not tomorrow but now,
  Our mail-day, today of the blood of the sweat of
    our brow,
The year of our war to the end. When and where we
    arrive
Is no matter, but *how* is the question we urgently need,
How to love and to hate, how to die, how to write and
    to read.

Sydney Bridge

Though I see you, O rainbow of iron and rivetted lace
As a dancer who leaps to the music of music and light,
And poised on the pin of the moment of marvelous grace
Holds her breath in the downfall and curve of her
motionless flight;

Though you walk like a queen with the stays of your
womanly steel
And the pearls of your bodice are heavy with sensual
pride,
And the million come under your notice and graciously
kneel,
As the navies of nations come slowly to moor at your side;

Yet your pace is the pace of a man's, and your arms are
outspread
In a trick of endurance to charm the demand of the bays,
And your tendons are common—the cables are coarse
on your head,

You are marxist and sweaty! You grind for the labor of
days;
And O sphinx of our harbor of beauty, your banner is red
And outflung at the end of the world like a silvery phrase!

Troop Train

It stops the town we come through. Workers raise
Their oily arms in good salute and grin.
Kids scream as at a circus. Business men
Glance hopefully and go their measured way.
And women standing at their dumbstruck door
More slowly wave and seem to warn us back,
As if a tear blinding the course of war
Might once dissolve our iron in their sweet wish.

Fruit of the world, O clustered on ourselves
We hang as from a cornucopia
In total friendliness, with faces bunched
To spray the streets with catcalls and with leers.
A bottle smashes on the moving ties
And eyes fixed on a lady smiling pink
Stretch like a rubber-band and snap and sting
The mouth that wants the drink-of-water kiss.

And on through crummy continents and days,
Deliberate, grimy, slightly drunk we crawl,
The good-bad boys of circumstance and chance,
Whose bucket-helmets bang the empty wall
Where twist the murdered bodies of our packs
Next to the guns that only seem themselves.
And distance like a strap adjusted shrinks,
Tightens across the shoulder and holds firm.

Here is a deck of cards; out of this hand
Dealer, deal me my luck, a pair of bulls,
The right draw to a flush, the one-eyed jack.
Diamonds and hearts are red but spades are black,
And spades are spades and clubs are clovers—black.
But deal me winners, souvenirs of peace.
This stands to reason and arithmetic,
Luck also travels and not all come back.

Trains lead to ships and ships to death or trains,
And trains to death or trucks, and trucks to death,
Or trucks lead to the march, the march to death,
Or that survival which is all our hope;
And death leads back to trucks and trains and ships,
But life leads to the march, O flag! at last
The place of life found after trains and death—
Nightfall of nations brilliant after war.

Christmas Eve: Australia

The wind blows hot. English and foreign birds
And insects different as their fish excite
The would-be calm. The usual flocks and herds
Parade in permanent quiet out of sight,
And there one crystal like a grain of light
Sticks in the crucible of day and cools.
A cloud burnt to a crisp at some great height
Sips at the dark condensing in deep pools.

I smoke and read my Bible and chew gum,
Thinking of Christ and Christmas of last year,

And what those quizzical soldiers standing near
Ask of the war and Christmases to come,
And sick of causes and the tremendous blame
Curse lightly and pronounce your serious name.

Full Moon: New Guinea

These nights we fear the aspects of the moon,
Sleep lightly in the radiance falling clear
On palms and ferns and hills and us; for soon
The small burr of the bombers in our ear
Tickles our rest; we rise as from a nap
And take our helmets absently and meet,
Prepared for any spectacle or mishap,
At trenches fresh and narrow at our feet.

Look up, look up, and wait and breathe. These nights
We fear Orion and the Cross. The crowd
Of deadly insects caught in our long lights
Glitter and seek to burrow in a cloud
Soft-mined with high explosive. Breathe and wait,
The bombs are falling darkly for our fate.

Sunday: New Guinea

The bugle sounds the measured call to prayers,
The band starts bravely with a clarion hymn,
From every side, singly, in groups, in pairs,
Each to his kind of service comes to worship Him.

Our faces washed, our hearts in the right place,
We kneel or stand or listen from our tents;
Half-naked natives with their kind of grace
Move down the road with balanced staffs like mendicants.

And over the hill the guns bang like a door
And planes repeat their mission in the heights.
The jungle outmaneuvers creeping war
And crawls within the circle of our sacred rites.

I long for our disheveled Sundays home,
Breakfast, the comics, news of latest crimes,
Talk without reference, and palindromes,
Sleep and the Philharmonic and the ponderous *Times*.

I long for lounging in the afternoons
Of clean intelligent warmth, my brother's mind,
Books and thin plates and flowers and shining
      spoons,
And your love's presence, snowy, beautiful, and kind.

Nigger

And did ever a man go black with sun in a Belgian swamp,
On a feathery African plain where the sunburnt lioness
      lies,
And a cocoanut monkey grove where the cockatoos
      scratch the skies,
And the zebras striped with moonlight grasses gaze and
      stomp?

With a swatch of the baboon's crimson bottom cut for
     a lip,
And a brace of elephant ivories hung for a tusky smile,
With the muscles as level and lazy and long as the lifting
     Nile,
And a penis as loaded and supple and limp as the slaver's
     whip?

Are you beautiful still when you walk downtown in a
     knife-cut coat
And your yellow shoes dance at the corner curb like a
     brand new car,
And the buck with the arching pick looks over the
     new-laid tar
As you cock your eye like a cuckoo bird on a
     two-o'clock note?

When you got so little in steel-rim specs, when you
     taught that French,
When you wrote that book and you made that speech in
     the bottom south,
When you beat that fiddle and sang that role for
     Othello's mouth,
When you blew that horn for the shirt-sleeve mob and
     the snaky wench?

When you boxed that hun, when you raped that trash
     that you didn't rape,
When you caught that slug with a belly of fire and a face
     of gray,

When you felt that loop and you took that boot from a
    KKK,
And your hands hung down and your face went out in a
    blast of grape?

Did the Lord say yes, did the Lord say no, did you ask
    the Lord
When the jaw came down, when the cotton blossomed
    out of your bones?
Are you coming to peace, O Booker T. Lincoln
    Roosevelt Jones,
And is Jesus riding to raise your wage and to cut that
    cord?

Franklin

The star of Reason, Ben, reposed in you
Octagon spectacles, a sparking kite,
Triggers and jiggers, bobbins, reels and screws,
And aphorisms spelled in black and white.

Wiseacre, editor, and diplomat,
First of the salesmen, hero of the clerk,
The logic of invention led to bells
Joyous for George and terrible for Burke.

Poor Richard prospers and the grocery man
Has your disarming prose and pays his tax.
Sir, what is the reason for this bird
That sings and screams and coos and crows and quacks?

Two-penny buns, a whistle for the boy,
Rare Ben, the printer's devil used you well.
Lenin and Freud embroider left and right
And Curtis beats The Independence Bell.

The Interlude

I

Much of transfiguration that we hear,
The ballet of the atoms, the second law
Of thermo-dynamics, Isis, and the queer

Fertilization of fish, the Catholic's awe
For the life-cycle of the Nazarene,
His wife whom sleeping Milton thought he saw;

Much of the resurrection that we've seen
And taken part in, like the Passion Play,
All of autumnal red and April green,

To those who walk in work from day to day,
To economic and responsible man,
All, all is substance. Life that lets him stay

Uses his substance kindly while she can
But drops him lifeless after his one span.

II

What lives? the proper creatures in their homes?
A weed? the white and giddy butterfly?
Bacteria? necklaces of chromosomes?

What lives? the breathing bell of the clear sky?
The crazed bull of the sea? Andean crags?
Armies that plunge into themselves to die?

People? A sacred relic wrapped in rags,
The ham-bone of a saint, the winter rose,
Do these?—And is there not a hand that drags

The bottom of the universe for those
Who still perhaps are breathing? Listen well,
There lives a quiet like a cathedral close

At the soul's center where substance cannot dwell
And life flowers like music from a bell.

III

Writing, I crushed an insect with my nail
And thought nothing at all. A bit of wing
Caught my eye then, a gossamer so frail

And exquisite, I saw in it a thing
That scorned the grossness of the thing I wrote.
It hung upon my finger like a sting.

A leg I noticed next, fine as a mote,
"And on this frail eyelash he walked," I said,
"And climbed and walked like any mountain-goat."

And in this mood I sought the little head,
But it was lost; then in my heart a fear
Cried out, "A life—why beautiful, why dead!"

It was a mite that held itself most dear,
So small I could have drowned it with a tear.

The Bed

Your clothes of snow and satin and pure blood
Are surplices of many sacraments
Full of the woven musk of birth and death,
Full of the wet wild-flower breath of marriages,
The sweat, the slow mandragora of lust.

Meadow of sleep, table of sour sickness,
Infinite road to travel, first of graves,
Your square and subtle presence rules the house,
And little wincing hurts of everyday
Clutch at your white skirt and are comforted.

What matter if you are wise or if you know?
A third of life is yours, all that we learn
We tell you, and you dream us night by night.

We take your advice, confess in sharp detail,
Add to your knowledge, yet can teach you nothing.
"Lie here," you say, and whoever we bring you, sad,
Ashamed or delighted, you take in the spirit we give.

Let me not know too much, and let your soul
Not lead me farther on than sleep and love,
For her I marry is more white than you.
Some day, as if with ancient torches stand
And fill the walls with fires around her head,
And let your gown be fresh as April grass,
And let your prothalamium be sweet.

The Synagogue

The synagogue dispirits the deep street,
Shadows the face of the pedestrian,
It is the adumbration of the Wall,
The stone survival that laments itself,
Our old entelechy of stubborn God,
Our calendar that marks a separate race.

The swift cathedral palpitates the blood,
The soul moves upward like a wing to meet
The pinnacles of saints. There flocks of thanks
In nooks of holy tracery arrive
And rested take their message in mid-air
Sphere after sphere into the papal heaven.

The altar of the Hebrews is a house,
No relic but a place, Sinai itself,
Not holy ground but factual holiness
Wherein the living god is resident.
Our scrolls are volumes of the thundered law
Sabbath by sabbath wound by hand to read.

He knows Al-Eloah to whom the Arab
Barefooted falls on sands, on table roofs,
In latticed alleys underneath the egg
On wide mosaics, when the crier shrills.
O profitable curse, most sacred rug,
Your book is blindness and your sword is rust.

And Judenhetze is the course of time;
We were rebellious, all but Abraham,
And skulked like Jonah, angry at the gourd.
Our days are captives in the minds of kings,
We stand in tens disjointed on the world
Grieving the ribbon of a coast we hated.

Some choose the ethics of belief beyond
Even particular election. Some
In bland memorial churches modify
The architecture of the state, and heaven
Disfranchised watches, caput mortuum,
The human substance eating, voting, smiling.

The Jew has no bedecked magnificat
But sits in stricken ashes after death,
Refusing grace; his grave is flowerless,

He gutters in the tallow of his name.
At Rome the multiplying tapers sing
Life endless in the history of art.

And Zion womanless refuses grace
To the first woman as to Magdalene,
But half-remembers Judith or Rahab,
The shrewd good heart of Esther honors still,
And weeps for almost sacred Ruth, but doubts
Either full harlotry or the faultless birth.

Our wine is wine, our bread is harvest bread
That feeds the body and is not the body.
Our blessing is to wine but not the blood
Nor to sangreal the sacred dish. We bless
The whiteness of the dish and bless the water
And are not anthropophagous to him.

The immanent son then came as one of us
And stood against the ark. We have no prophets,
Our scholars are afraid. There have been friars,
Great healers, poets. The stars were terrible.
At the Sadducee court he touched our panic;
We were betrayed to sacrifice this man.

We live by virtue of philosophy,
Past love, and have our devious reward.
For faith he gave us land and took the land,
Thinking us exiles of all humankind.
Our name is yet the identity of God
That storms the falling altar of the world.

Birthday Poem

Five hundred nights and days ago
We kissed goodbye at the iron gates
Of the terminal, two of a crowd of twos,
Half of us mobbed away below
Where the engine pants and pants and waits,
Half of us trailing back in the snow
In taxis and cars to wait for news,
And like an enormous sign, a pair
Of blurred lips hung in the smoky air.

So far, so long, what can I say
To help commemorate your today,
What can I ever give to prove,
If proof were ever needed, love?
We are too used to words; we think
In terms of Anna, Virginia Woolf,
At times approach that dreaded brink
And stare into the selfsame gulf
That drew their splendid souls away.

We are too rich with books, our blood
Is heavy with over-thoughtful food,
Our minds are gravid—and yet to try
To backtrack to simplicity
Is fatal. Every Walden fails;
Those cynical ladies of Versailles
With silken frocks and silver pails
Playing at milkmaid sicken us.
We have our war to quicken us.

Still to be proud, still to be neat
Of smile and phrase is not for us.
The ladies of *Vogue* so vacuous,
The lips well-tailored and effete
Belong to a world that never was;
And—not to test the extremes of Swift—
The *inter faeces et urinas*
Comes to my mind, however sweet
The token of a birthday gift.

Far from the ads of gloss and glass
Of all the cities of East and West,
Today I carved with a jungle knife
An artefact of the native class,
As innocent, undemonstrative.
Blisters, sandpaper, and the best
Of scanty craftsmanship I give,
A bit of lumber cut from life,
And not to be called a primitive.

Things we step over, stones we kick
How often excel in perfect form
The treasures of miles of galleries.
I send you, darling, a polished stick
To open letters, hold in your hand.
The lovely markings smooth and warm
Grew in a palm by silent seas;
Forests of uncut trinkets stand
In groves of already perfect trees.

My trinket is more than a kiss and less,
More than a hand's twofold caress,

More than the journey it must make
Thousands of miles for remembrance' sake,
More than the world-encircling pang,
And less than the world from which it sprang,
Less than the journeying I've seen,
Less than the war of red and green,
Less than the total love I mean.

The Leg

Among the iodoform, in twilight-sleep,
What have I lost? he first inquires,
Peers in the middle distance where a pain,
Ghost of a nurse, hazily moves, and day,
Her blinding presence pressing in his eyes
And now his ears. They are handling him
With rubber hands. He wants to get up.

One day beside some flowers near his nose
He will be thinking, *When will I look at it?*
And pain, still in the middle distance, will reply,
At what? and he will know it's gone,
O where! and begin to tremble and cry.
He will begin to cry as a child cries
Whose puppy is mangled under a screaming wheel.

Later, as if deliberately, his fingers
Begin to explore the stump. He learns a shape
That is comfortable and tucked in like a sock.
This has a sense of humor, this can despise
The finest surgical limb, the dignity of limping,

The nonsense of wheel-chairs. Now he smiles to the wall:
The amputation becomes an acquisition.

For the leg is wondering where he is (all is not lost)
And surely he has a duty to the leg;
He is its injury, the leg is his orphan,
He must cultivate the mind of the leg,
Pray for the part that is missing, pray for peace
In the image of man, pray, pray for its safety,
And after a little it will die quietly.

The body, what is it, Father, but a sign
To love the force that grows us, to give back
What in Thy palm is senselessness and mud?
Knead, knead the substance of our understanding
Which must be beautiful in flesh to walk,
That if Thou take me angrily in hand
And hurl me to the shark, I shall not die!

Movie

While you arrange yourself and set your eyes
Like spectacles upon your nose,
Out of the cool contented dark the long
Aeolian gales of music rise
And finger at your nerves; the data flows
Evenly upward with the names of hands,
The dress designer, master of decor,
Historian and lyric writer, bands,
The cast, the great Director. Then no more.

The silence mediates the pause, then flings
The window of your interest
Wide open on the street. Lean out and look,
He's coming! he's the guy who brings
That book to life exactly as you guessed;
Goodlooking too, all over kisses, clean,
And knows how to behave; he'll never die;
They'll save him for the close-up closing scene;
We want it that way; all of us know why.

A woman sits beside you, so intent
You'd think she was a breathless child;
Your knee is touching hers, light as a nod;
She'll wonder later what it meant
Because she didn't mind; it was a mild
Impersonal pressure, curiously polite,
Dim as the Exit sign upon the wall.
Outside she wouldn't even glance goodnight—
Perhaps you haven't touched her after all.

But up there she has cast her simple spell:
Sweet mouth, sweet eyes, sweet angry hair,
Chiaroscuro flawless as the moon,
Round as the face of Raphael.
O blond of mortal instinct, if we stare,
Let us; we tell you secrets that we dream
Of you, Astarte! (for we know your past).
But now in the dark be only what you seem,
Sugar us with your kisses while you last.

The world swallows your pill, quack that it is,
And loves it. Yes, it works a cure,

It makes us turn our heads, like smelling salts;
We think, *We'll go slow after this.*
It was terrific: or perhaps more sure
Of what's unreal, Inside or Out, we sight
A skirt, and with an intimating cough
Follow it down the street; or else we light
A cigarette, and start to walk it off.

Elegy for a Dead Soldier

I

A white sheet on the tail-gate of a truck
Becomes an altar; two small candlesticks
Sputter at each side of the crucifix
Laid round with flowers brighter than the blood,
Red as the red of our apocalypse,
Hibiscus that a marching man will pluck
To stick into his rifle or his hat,
And great blue morning-glories pale as lips
That shall no longer taste or kiss or swear.
The wind begins a low magnificat,
The chaplain chats, the palmtrees swirl their hair,
The columns come together through the mud.

II

We too are ashes as we watch and hear
The psalm, the sorrow, and the simple praise
Of one whose promised thoughts of other days
Were such as ours, but now wholly destroyed,

The service record of his youth wiped out,
His dream dispersed by shot, must disappear.
What can we feel but wonder at a loss
That seems to point at nothing but the doubt
Which flirts our sense of luck into the ditch?
Reader of Paul who prays beside this fosse,
Shall we believe our eyes or legends rich
With glory and rebirth beyond the void?

III

For this comrade is dead, dead in the war,
A young man out of millions yet to live,
One cut away from all that war can give,
Freedom of self and peace to wander free.
Who mourns in all this sober multitude
Who did not feel the bite of it before
The bullet found its aim? This worthy flesh,
This boy laid in a coffin and reviewed—
Who has not wrapped himself in this same flag,
Heard the light fall of dirt, his wound still fresh,
Felt his eyes closed, and heard the distant brag
Of the last volley of humanity?

IV

By chance I saw him die, stretched on the ground,
A tattooed arm lifted to take the blood
Of someone else sealed in a tin. I stood
During the last delirium that stays
The intelligence a tiny moment more,
And then the strangulation, the last sound.

The end was sudden, like a foolish play,
A stupid fool slamming a foolish door,
The absurd catastrophe, half-prearranged,
And all the decisive things still left to say.
So we disbanded, angrier and unchanged,
Sick with the utter silence of dispraise.

V

We ask for no statistics of the killed,
For nothing political impinges on
This single casualty, or all those gone,
Missing or healing, sinking or dispersed,
Hundreds of thousands counted, millions lost.
More than an accident and less than willed
Is every fall, and this one like the rest.
However others calculate the cost,
To us the final aggregate is *one*,
One with a name, one transferred to the blest;
And though another stoops and takes the gun,
We cannot add the second to the first.

VI

I would not speak for him who could not speak
Unless my fear were true: he was not wronged,
He knew to which decision he belonged
But let it choose itself. Ripe in instinct,
Neither the victim nor the volunteer,
He followed, and the leaders could not seek
Beyond the followers. Much of this he knew;
The journey was a detour that would steer

Into the Lincoln Highway of a land
Remorselessly improved, excited, new,
And that was what he wanted. He had planned
To earn and drive. He and the world had winked.

VII

No history deceived him, for he knew
Little of times and armies not his own;
He never felt that peace was but a loan,
Had never questioned the idea of gain.
Beyond the headlines once or twice he saw
The gathering of a power by the few
But could not tell their names; he cast his vote,
Distrusting all the elected but not law.
He laughed at socialism; *on mourrait*
Pour les industriels? He shed his coat
And not for brotherhood, but for his pay.
To him the red flag marked the sewer main.

VIII

Above all else he loathed the homily,
The slogan and the ad. He paid his bill,
But not for Congressmen at Bunker Hill.
Ideals were few and those there were not made
For conversation. He belonged to church
But never spoke of God. The Christmas tree,
The Easter egg, baptism, he observed,
Never denied the preacher on his perch,
And would not sign Resolved That or Whereas.
Softness he had and hours and nights reserved

For thinking, dressing, dancing to the jazz.
His laugh was real, his manners were homemade.

IX

Of all men poverty pursued him least;
He was ashamed of all the down and out,
Spurned the panhandler like an uneasy doubt,
And saw the unemployed as a vague mass
Incapable of hunger or revolt.
He hated other races, south or east,
And shoved them to the margin of his mind.
He could recall the justice of the Colt,
Take interest in a gang-war like a game.
His ancestry was somewhere far behind
And left him only his peculiar name.
Doors opened, and he recognized no class.

X

His children would have known a heritage,
Just or unjust, the richest in the world,
The quantum of all art and science curled
In the horn of plenty, bursting from the horn,
A people bathed in honey, Paris come,
Vienna transferred with the highest wage,
A World's Fair spread to Phoenix, Jacksonville,
Earth's capital, the new Byzantium,
Kingdom of man—who knows? Hollow or firm,
No man can ever prophesy until
Out of our death some undiscovered germ,
Whole toleration or pure peace is born.

XI

The time to mourn is short that best becomes
The military dead. We lift and fold the flag,
Lay bare the coffin with its written tag,
And march away. Behind, four others wait
To lift the box, the heaviest of loads.
The anesthetic afternoon benumbs,
Sickens our senses, forces back our talk.
We know that others on tomorrow's roads
Will fall, ourselves perhaps, the man beside,
Over the world the threatened, all who walk:
And could we mark the grave of him who died
We would write this beneath his name and date:

EPITAPH

Underneath this wooden cross there lies
A Christian killed in battle. You who read,
Remember that this stranger died in pain;
And passing here, if you can lift your eyes
Upon a peace kept by a human creed,
Know that one soldier has not died in vain.

Crusoe

Shocked by the naked footprint in the sand
His heart thumps in a panic; he looks away
Beyond the curve of the last spur of the land,
Searches the reef where combers boom and spray;

And shouldering his gun, his English dog
Running beside, returns to his clean cave,
The precious cask of tools, the written log,
The parrot, his rocker on its barrel stave.

He says a prayer. The years of silence hear.
He shall be answered with a man. To learn,
To laugh, to teach, to feel a presence near,
Share his beloved resourcefulness and return.

For he has outwitted nature and shipwreck;
Some day the tapering mast will fill the west,
The castaway once more upon the deck
Gaze at two worlds, and set sail for the best.

Gladly he gives this isle to all mankind
To tread the hills and shores with countless feet.
Henceforth the globe itself swims in his mind,
The last unknown and insular retreat.

The Intellectual

What should the wars do with these jigging fools?

The man behind the book may not be man,
His own man or the book's or yet the time's,
But still be whole, deciding what he can
In praise of politics or German rimes;

But the intellectual lights a cigarette
And offers it lit to the lady, whose odd smile
Is the merest hyphen—lest he should forget
What he has been resuming all the while.

He talks to overhear, she to withdraw
To some interior feminine fireside
Where the back arches, beauty puts forth a paw
Like a black puma stretching in velvet pride,

Making him think of cats, a stray of which
Some days sets up a howling in his brain,
Pure interference such as this neat bitch
Seems to create from listening disdain.

But talk is all the value, the release,
Talk is the very fillip of an act,
The frame and subject of the masterpiece
Under whose film of age the face is cracked.

His own forehead glows like expensive wood,
But back of it the mind is disengaged,
Self-sealing clock recording bad and good
At constant temperature, intact, unaged.

But strange, his body is an open house
Inviting every passerby to stay;
The city to and fro beneath his brows
Wanders and drinks and chats from night to day.

Think of a private thought, indecent room
Where one might kiss his daughter before bed!
Life is embarrassed; shut the family tomb,
Console your neighbor for his recent dead;

Do something! die in Spain or paint a green
Gouache, go into business (Rimbaud did),
Or start another Little Magazine,
Or move in with a woman, have a kid.

Invulnerable, impossible, immune,
Do what you will, your will will not be done
But dissipate the light of afternoon
Till evening flickers like the midnight sun,

And midnight shouts and dies: I'd rather be
A milkman walking in his sleep at dawn
Bearing fat quarts of cream, and so be free,
Crossing alone and cold from lawn to lawn.

I'd rather be a barber and cut hair
Than walk with you in gilt museum halls,
You and the puma-lady, she so rare
Exhaling her silk soul upon the walls.

Go take yourselves apart, but let me be
The fault you find with everyman. I spit,
I laugh, I fight; and you, *l'homme qui rît*;
Swallow your stale saliva, and still sit.

Spider

I envy you, Arachne, painted, fat,
Swaying in the center of your silky snare,
Mending and weaving your welcome mat,
Sultry sultana, alone, in league
With nothing on earth but your lovely hair,
And the latest victim of your last intrigue.

Center of interest of all your designs,
Your craft is ageless, cynical, appalling,
Pencilling on nothing your silver lines,
Gathering and kissing the captured lives.
What a jewel you are! I can see you crawling
On the breast of one of Baudelaire's wives.

Satire: Anxiety

Alas, I would be overloved,
A sign, a Wonder unreproved,
A bronze colossus standing high
As Rhodes or famous Liberty,
Bridging with my almighty thighs
A stainless-steel metropolis
Where pigmy men in clothing creep
To Lilliputian work and sleep,
And Love with microscopic tears
Whispers to wee and perfect ears.
I would obscure the sun and throw
A shadow with my smallest toe

That down their teeming canyon files
Time could be told a hundred miles;
Lightning would flash within my hand,
An airman's beacon and sign of land,
My eyes eclipse the polar star,
Aldebaran and the flare of war;
Golden my head and cleanly hewn
Would sail above the lesser moon
And dart above the Pleiades
To peer at new astronomies
From where the earth, a bluish clod,
Seems smallest in the eye of God.

But when in lucid morning I
Survey my bulk and history,
Composite fool alive in air
With caecum and vestigial hair,
A thing of not-too-godly form
Conversant with the waiting worm,
Fixed in a span between two shades
For four or five or six decades,
Then all my pride and all my hope
As backward through a telescope
Diminish: I walk an endless street
Where topless towers for height compete,
And men of wiser blood and bone
Destroy me for the things they own—
Their taxes, vital tubes, and sons
Submissive in a world of guns.
I see my hands grow small and clear
Until they wink and disappear.

V-Letter

I love you first because your face is fair,
>Because your eyes Jewish and blue,
Set sweetly with the touch of foreignness
Above the cheekbones, stare rather than dream.
Often your countenance recalls a boy
>Blue-eyed and small, whose silent mischief
Tortured his parents and compelled my hate
>>To wish his ugly death.
Because of this reminder, my soul's trouble,
And for your face, so often beautiful,
>>I love you, wish you life.

I love you first because you wait, because
>For your own sake, I cannot write
Beyond these words. I love you for these words
That sting and creep like insects and leave filth.
I love you for the poverty you cry
>And I bend down with tears of steel
That melt your hand like wax, not for this war
>>The droplets shattering
Those candle-glowing fingers of my joy,
But for your name of agony, my love,
>>That cakes my mouth with salt.

And all your imperfections and perfections
>And all your magnitude of grace
And all this love explained and unexplained
Is just a breath. I see you woman-size
And this looms larger and more goddess-like

Than silver goddesses on screens.
I see you in the ugliness of light,
                    Yet you are beautiful,
And in the dark of absence your full length
Is such as meets my body to the full
                    Though I am starved and huge.

You turn me from these days as from a scene
                    Out of an open window far
Where lies the foreign city and the war.
You are my home and in your spacious love
I dream to march as under flaring flags
                    Until the door is gently shut.
Give me the tearless lesson of your pride,
                    Teach me to live and die
As one deserving anonymity,
The mere devotion of a house to keep
                    A woman and a man.

Give me the free and poor inheritance
                    Of our own kind, not furniture
Of education, nor the prophet's pose,
The general cause of words, the hero's stance,
The ambitions incommensurable with flesh,
                    But the drab makings of a room
Where sometimes in the afternoon of thought
                    The brief and blinding flash
May light the enormous chambers of your will
And show the gracious Parthenon that time
                    Is ever measured by.

As groceries in a pantry gleam and smile
      Because they are important weights
Bought with the metal minutes of your pay,
So do these hours stand in solid rows,
The dowry for a use in common life.
      I love you first because your years
Lead to my matter-of-fact and simple death
      Or to our open marriage,
And I pray nothing for my safety back,
Not even luck, because our love is whole
      Whether I live or fail.

Resultantly, all that once had seemed inherent
And lawful in composition now appeared
Not stale but actually incoherent. Form
Became the atoms that bombard the senses;
The composer became a compositor; the line
Crumbled to bits of syllable, and design
All but supplanted count of eye and ear;
Until the day arrived when many a poet
Sat with a lapful of pied type and lead
And puzzled over the fragments, while some few
Descanted on the attraction of the new.

BREAKDOWN
OF METRIC

———

I do not here attempt the definition
Of rime, which is the province of esthetics,
But to point out its ratio to language.
In the mathematical sense, rime is a power,
Prose raised to the numerical exponent
Of three or six or even n, depending
Upon the propensity of the literature
At a particular time and on the bent
Of the particular poet. It is therefore

THE RATIO
OF RIME TO
LANGUAGE

A heightening and a measure of intensity.
In the physical sense, rime is the nuclear
And vital element of speech and prose,
The very protoplasm of the tongue,
Or that organic substance which survives
The structures it creates. Words are as lives,
Deaths and mutations, and the poet learns
Through search for life, the biology of rime.
In the theological sense, rime is the ghost
And prose the flesh of language. Poets may boast
That they have known the mystic rose of good,
The blessed face of truth, the host of beauty;
They press the oil and elevate the wine,
For poetry like philosophy is divine
And wells up from the uncreated will.

———

                    In every age of rime
Poets have employed constructions of their own,
Useless to prose, inversion being the chief
Of these. Not till the present century
Was it thought necessary to avoid
Such an expedient and to conform
Wholly to the syntax of conversation.
In part we lay our reaction at the door
Of the Victorian and Edwardian tribe
Whose influence penetrated to the last
Georgian. Inversion suddenly saw itself

A Dorian Gray, a monster in disguise.
One can indeed condone the indignation
Of the early moderns; when we consider Dowson
Twisting his grief into a villanelle,
We feel embarrassment. "Fruits and flowers among"
To our more literal ear seems better left
Unsaid. Yet is it just as well that rime
Rejects the entire principle of inversion?   INVERSION
I think not, for in poetry half the magic
Lies in the balance of the phrase. When Auden
Writes "Call us not tragic" he reclaims
A form not only dear to art but new.
Correctness dulls, precision often maims
The poem; nor can the grammar rule the rime;
It is the poem that sets the grammar right.

———

Perhaps it is that Poe was the last poet
In the classic signification of the word;
Europe was quick to claim the furniture   THE POETRY
Of his rich vision (and the sticks and props   OF VISION
With which he stuffed his mansion) but the bird,
The princess, Helen herself, were dead.
Recumbent Poe before the deep backdrops
Became the Lenin of the Symbolists;
The yeast of criticism worked, and rime
Declined to verbiage, decomposed to forms.
The greatest of the logical suicides

During that century of fermenting art
Witnessed the great confusion and vowed silence;
This was Rimbaud, in whom the broken cry
To purify the word echoes the prayer
Of Baudelaire to purify the heart.

Nor is it any accident that Emerson
Anointed Whitman and not Poe. The nation
A hundred years ago was real estate
For the synthetic myth and poetry
On the grand national-international scale.
I do not think that I exaggerate
In saying that our period has produced
More poems conceived as epics, large and small,
Than has the entire history of rime!
The bulk of these fall from the sanguine pens
Of Emersonian and Whitmanian bards;
These in their works, as if to justify
And prove our transcendental unity,
Recite the whole geography and construct
A gigantic stage perennially set
For some Siegfried who never comes.

Homecoming

Lost in the vastness of the void Pacific
My thousand days of exile, pain,
Bid me farewell. Gone is the Southern Cross
To her own sky, fallen a continent
Under the wave, dissolved the bitterest isles
In their salt element,
And here upon the deck the mist encloses
My smile that would light up all darkness
And ask forgiveness of the things that thrust
Shame and all death on millions and on me.

We bring no raw materials from the East
But green-skinned men in blue-lit holds
And lunatics impounded between-decks;
The mighty ghoul-ship that we ride exhales
The sickly-sweet stench of humiliation,
And even the majority, untouched by steel
Or psychoneurosis, stare with eyes in rut,
Their hands a rabble to snatch the riches
Of glittering shops and girls.

Because I am angry at this kindness which
Is both habitual and contradictory
To the life of armies, now I stand alone

And hate the swarms of khaki men that crawl
Like lice upon the wrinkled hide of earth,
Infesting ships as well. Not otherwise
Could I lean outward piercing fog to find
Our sacred bridge of exile and return.
My tears are psychological, not poems
To the United States; my smile is prayer.

Gnawing the thin slops of anxiety,
Escorted by the groundswell and by gulls,
In silence and with mystery we enter
The territorial waters. Not till then
Does that convulsive terrible joy, more sudden
And brilliant than the explosion of a ship,
Shatter the tensions of the heaven and sea
To crush a hundred thousand skulls
And liberate in that high burst of love
The imprisoned souls of soldiers and of me.

Demobilization

Forty-nine men and I stand at attention
In Maryland, at the dead center of peace,
Lean and prepared to give the last salute
And graduate from war. Within this square
I am somewhere but difficult to find,
As in a photograph of graduation
Where youth predominates and looks alive.
Here youth predominates and eyes are veined
And strained. This is the Class of 'Forty-five.

The tattered flag that snaps upon the mast
Like a fine hound upon a leash, the horn
That croaks tired announcements to the wind,
Barracks that split and need a coat of paint,
The exhausted colonel shaking hands with me,
The dusty clouds and rather puzzled sun
All drearily perform. Only the small
Recruits, the babies of no war at all,
Move with an appetite to please and learn.

Dimly it comes to me that this is home,
This is my Maryland, these pines I know,
This camp itself when budding green and raw
I watched in agony of shame. Then quick
To disobey, today it is my law,
The school that coming back to I forgive.
Safe in the pacifism of return
Will I lie down and play the wounded man
And smile at information and drink deep.

There will my wife penelopize and teach
Such love as liquefies adulterous man;
There will my mother often touch my hand
As if my hand were nearly out of reach;
My friends also, sure they have lost a friend,
Will shiftily in conversation span
The years of separation. Less than the same,
Same things will burden every mind, and peace
In the poor victorious logic of our kind

Take form. About me stands the brotherhood
Imposed by tragedy from overhead;
The pattern is about to wrench and break,
And that itself is victory and good.
Let the evilly perfect fifties fall,
Deteriorate into all separate men,
All free, all loyal to themselves, all glad;
Let the smart hand come down, never to rise,
And all who can go back to what they had.

We are running wildly, boys in June, gunmen
Paroled, rabbits let loose, no one to follow!
We fly with the full frenzy of escape
Down highways fallen into disrepair,
Past merchants trading in insignia,
The childish heraldry of grownup war.
Saviors and spies, we seek the road we lost
When kidnapped from indifference. As before,
Back where I started from, I stare, touch wood.

The Conscientious Objector

The gates clanged and they walked you into jail
More tense than felons but relieved to find
The hostile world shut out, the flags that dripped
From every mother's windowpane, obscene
The bloodlust sweating from the public heart,
The dog authority slavering at your throat.
A sense of quiet, of pulling down the blind
Possessed you. Punishment you felt was clean.

The decks, the catwalks, and the narrow light
Composed a ship. This was a mutinous crew
Troubling the captains for plain decencies,
A Mayflower brim with pilgrims headed out
To establish new theocracies to west,
A Noah's ark coasting the topmost seas
Ten miles above the sodomites and fish.
These inmates loved the only living doves.

Like all men hunted from the world you made
A good community, voyaging the storm
To no safe Plymouth or green Ararat;
Trouble or calm, the men with Bibles prayed,
The gaunt politicals construed our hate.
The opposite of all armies, you were best
Opposing uniformity and yourselves;
Prison and personality were your fate.

You suffered not so physically but knew
Maltreatment, hunger, ennui of the mind.
Well might the soldier kissing the hot beach
Erupting in his face damn all your kind.
Yet you who saved neither yourselves nor us
Are equally with those who shed the blood
The heroes of our cause. Your conscience is
What we come back to in the armistice.

The Convert

Deep in the shadowy bethel of the tired mind,
Where spooks and death lights ride, and Marys, too,
Materialize like senseless ectoplasm
Smiling in blue, out of the blue,
Quite gradually, on a common afternoon,
With no more inner fanfare than a sigh,
With no cross in the air, drizzle of blood,
Beauty of blinding voices from up high,
The man surrenders reason to the ghost
And enters church, via the vestry room.

The groan of positive science, hiss of friends,
Substantiate what doctors call
His rather shameful and benign disease,
But ecumenical heaven clearly sees
His love, his possibilities.
O victory of the Unintelligence,
What mystic rose developing from rock
Is more a miracle than this overthrow?
What Constitution ever promised more
Than his declared insanity?

Yet he shall be less perfect than before,
Being no longer neutral to the Book
But answerable. What formerly were poems,
Precepts, and commonplaces now are laws,
Dantean atlases, and official news.
The dust of ages settles on his mind
And in his ears he hears the click of beads

Adding, adding, adding like a prayer machine
His heartfelt sums. Upon his new-found knees
He treasures up the gold of never-ending day.

All arguments are vain—that Notre Dame
Has plumbing, Baptists shoot their fellowmen,
Hindus are pious, nuns have Cadillacs.
Apologetics anger him who is
The living proof of what he newly knows;
And proudly sorrowing for those who fail
To read his simple summa theologica,
He prays that in the burning they be spared,
And prays for mercy as the south wind blows,
And for all final sins that tip the scale.

Peace on a hundred thousand temples falls
With gently even light, revealing some
With wounded walls and missing faces, some
Spared by the bombardier, and some by God.
In mournful happiness the clerics move
To put the altars back, and the new man,
Heartbroken, walks among the broken saints,
Thinking how heavy is the hand that hates,
How light and secret is the sign of love
In the hour of many significant conversions.

An Urn of Ashes

I bring an urn of ashes for all those
Who come into the presence of love's death
To be unmarried and to curse the rose

That swore so beautifully to live the years.
What god is there with large eyes of dismay
Who broods over the death of marriages?

Alas, there is no god, but a bare judge,
The scholar of dry perjury who leafs
Through books of yellow buckram to discern
Old woes and precedents of woes;
This is the man who manumits our souls
And knows that laws are never to the rose.

Neither the god's priest, mealy-mouthed and suave,
Nor the sad god of divorce can really save
These people. Angrily opposed they stand
And put between them the slick table top.
They are like heirs assembled in a room
To hear the dreadful treatise of a will.

Until from the dry lips of the learned man
There falls a stale flat flower of the law,
Some old kiss pressed into a book of torts
That got there by a foolish sentiment.
This is awarded to the wife.
The husband is awarded a blunt knife.

Nervously now he does what he is told
—To plunge the instrument into her life,
And that is all. They separate, they live,
At first in rooms with covered mirrors, then
In bright apartments where the newness hides
An urn of ashes in a plaster cope.

V

My first small book was nourished in the dark,
Secretly written, published, and inscribed.
Bound in wine-red, it made no brilliant mark.
Rather impossible relatives subscribed.

The best review was one I wrote myself
Under the name of a then-dearest friend.
Two hundred volumes stood upon my shelf
Saying my golden name from end to end.

I was not proud but seriously stirred;
Sorrow was song and money poetry's maid!
Sorrow I had in many a ponderous word,
But were the piper and the printer paid?

VII

The third-floor thoughts of discontented youth
Once saw the city, hardened against truth,
Get set for war. He coupled a last rime
And waited for the summons to end time.

It came. The box-like porch where he had sat,
The four bright boxes of a medium flat,
Chair he had sat in, glider where he lay
Reading the poets and prophets of his day,

He assigned abstractly to his dearest friend,
Glanced at the little street hooked at the end,
The line of poplars lately touched with spring,
Lovely as Laura, breathless, beckoning.

Mother was calm, until he left the door;
The trolley passed his sweetheart's house before
She was awake. The armory was cold,
But naked, shivering, shocked he was enrolled.

It was the death he never quite forgot
Through the four years of death, and like as not
The true death of the best of all of us
Whose present life is largely posthumous.

    x

I lost my father in a dire divorce,
My father lost I lost my ordered mind
And fell into high Christian intercourse
And face to face came with an ancient force.
To wicked spirits are horrid shapes assigned.

Men died at my feet and iron fell
From nowhere, iron from the zodiac.
One time the python of the oracle
Appeared before my tent.—Immanuel,
Done is a battell on the dragon blak!

I had no joy in any man who thought
Seeing what things the darker eye divined,
But dragged my reason toward the richest-wrought,

Three-towered and Christian-crusted juggernaut.
To wicked spirits are horrid shapes assigned.

Two priests advised me on my rise to grace,
The one among the sacred bric-a-brac
Questioning my devotion to my face,
The other frankly dubious of my race.
Done is a battell on the dragon blak.

I craved the beads and chains of paradise
And counted it a blessing to go blind;
Small truths alone I saw with open eyes
For in the blackest night was my sunrise.
To wicked spirits are horrid shapes assigned.

God's book was in my blood, I was confined
To fifty thousand years upon His rack
And no middle direction could I find.
To wicked spirits are horrid shapes assigned;
Done is a battell on the dragon blak.

XII

I plucked the bougainvillaea
      In Queensland in time of war;
The train stopped at the station
      And I reached it from my door.

I have never kept a flower
      And this one I never shall
I thought as I laid the blossom
      In the leaves of *Les Fleurs du Mal.*

I read my book in the desert
    In the time of death and fear,
The flower slipped from the pages
    And fell to my lap, my dear.

I sent it inside my letter,
    The purplest kiss I knew,
And thus you abused my passion
    With "A most Victorian Jew."

XVI

The atheist bride is dressed in blue,
The heretic groom in olive-drab,
The rabbi, of more somber hue,
Arrives upon the scene by cab.

A brief injunction to the pair
With no talk of the demiurge
Gives them the gist of the affair;
They sign the contract and emerge.

The witnesses on silent feet
Follow into the vestry hall;
The English text is short and sweet,
The Hebrew almost not at all.

A tendency to faint concludes
The sacrament. The atmosphere
Heavy with memory extrudes
From every second eye a tear.

A dinner laid for fifty-odd
Takes place in public, with champagne;
The heretic groom assumes the god,
Resists the need to be profane.

The tribal victim dressed in blue
Plans the escape. Disqualified
From the penultimate interview,
No maids of honor bed the bride.

The class that he had always curst
Thus circumvents the angry groom;
He and the atheist, reversed,
Are locked into a hotel room.

The God of the Old Testament
Is locked into the stately ark;
Hymen's attentions are well meant
But marriage happens in the dark.

The Dirty Word

The dirty word hops in the cage of the mind like the
Pondicherry vulture, stomping with its heavy left claw on
the sweet meat of the brain and tearing it with its vicious
beak, ripping and chopping the flesh. Terrified, the small
boy bears the big bird of the dirty word into the house, and
grunting, puffing, carries it up the stairs to his own room in
the skull. Bits of black feather cling to his clothes and his
hair as he locks the staring creature in the dark closet.

All day the small boy returns to the closet to examine and feed the bird, to caress and kick the bird, that now snaps and flaps its wings savagely whenever the door is opened. How the boy trembles and delights at the sight of the white excrement of the bird! How the bird leaps and rushes against the walls of the skull, trying to escape from the zoo of the vocabulary! How wildly snaps the sweet meat of the brain in its rage.

And the bird outlives the man, being freed at the man's death-funeral by a word from the rabbi.

But I one morning went upstairs and opened the door and entered the closet and found in the cage of my mind the great bird dead. Softly I wept it and softly removed it and softly buried the body of the bird in the hollyhock garden of the house I lived in twenty years before. And out of the worn black feathers of the wing have I made pens to write these elegies, for I have outlived the bird, and I have murdered it in my early manhood.

Words for a Child's Birthday

Finally I understand the meaning of birthdays,
      who somewhere in my teens despaired
      of celebrating the passing of time,
the fuss of the hour, the momentary blaze
      of attention. Then I was unprepared
to stop for events: on the other hand must climb
to where events were far away and dead
      and finally the eye could rest
      clearly above and see time spread
nicely below, the world made whole and manifest.

Because you were born this day a year ago
     I understand the passing of time
     and will try to arrest it, and thank God
that this one year was wonderful and slow,
   bringing you to the very prime
of infancy. Learning your seventh word
and your seventh step you have already crossed
     millions of years of intelligence,
     time forever and never lost
to the angels and apes who gave you this pre-eminence.

I write this down as if you could understand
     the silly motivations of fathers
     or the cause of words or the click of night.
I write you from an older wonderland
     where colors tire and dust gathers
on even favorite works. My troglodyte,
my fish fished out of darkness by a scream,
     do you prefer dry land to the warm
     salt mother-ocean of your dream
in which you swam to learn your perfect final form?

I note you do. Human by leaps and bounds,
     each day you lose a little love
     for night, just as the aged lose
a little love for day. Yes, you have grounds
     for waking like a cock to prove
that day is ready. Wake then and accuse,
wake and demand and shake your little jail,
     drive the groggy giants in,
     wag the dragons by the tail
until the world and time rattle like brilliant tin!

Then have no reverence for the different two,
    the agents, feeders, bodyguards
    of your survival and your play
who grow serious merely by owning you,
    straining like twin camelopards
over your life, and turning slightly gray—
composite spirit and sprite, subliminal,
    seminal, recently fish, pig,
    frog, snake, germ, physical
thought, but finally daughter, beautiful, startling, big.

Air Liner

Man has devised his ugliest claptrap
In this machine; a boxcar with a wing,
A wing in which lie bolted and concealed
Two automobiles or four. Electric fans
Of monstrous size project. Up in the nose
The pilot squats, the brain of the insect.
The rudder, most ridiculous fin, sticks up
Behind, a kind of billboard. Nothing fits.

But suddenly the fans are on, a gale
Begins beneath the wheels. Pivoting
We gawk and turkey-trot to the wide road
Laid out for this, and pausing, gather strength
For the grand leap. The earth flows to a blur,
The senses roar and, multiplying might,
Lean to the onrush, tilting up the tail,
Straining to lift us, blunder us upstairs.

Without delay we fly. The bottom drops
Out of the world and houses shrink to scale;
River and town slow to a walking pace,
Nursery objects, models for a war
Upon a general's table.—Why are we bored?
Why is it nothing new? And is there no
Sensation of the height? It's getting cold,
It slips, it skids, it bumps us like a truck.

Outside the wind is pulling bits of cloud
From infinite wool fields. Suddenly we are blind,
Wrapped in cocoons of nothingness far over
The ever-lost, the ever-wished-for earth.
Our boxcar drifts from time, and in the front
A small door opens and reveals a man
At a typewriter, writing what, to whom?
Soon we must die or plunge to death or freeze.

One with his dials and clocks is hauling us
Like fools around the firmament, and one
Sits at a sky desk writing. Both are mad,
Both are the baggage men of our good souls.
And yet we trust these young and lunatic
Mechanics with our lives, who should have been
Bus drivers shifting gears from street to street,
Nodding good morning, chewing, making change.

O reap the brilliants of the sky and climb,
Truck-driver poet! Your secret name I know,
You and your awkward bird with gilded beak,
Your pitiable unbending hawk, your iron

Soaring eagle. Man with the strength of hand
To hold these tons of flesh and steel aloft,
You are the white Icarian arm of man's
Escape from man into the electric Sun.

The Progress of Faust

He was born in Deutschland, as you would suspect,
And graduated in magic from Cracow
In Fifteen Five. His portraits show a brow
Heightened by science. The eye is indirect,
As of bent light upon a crooked soul,
And that he bargained with the Prince of Shame
For pleasures intellectually foul
Is known by every court that lists his name.

His frequent disappearances are put down
To visits in the regions of the damned
And to the periodic deaths he shammed,
But, unregenerate and in Doctor's gown,
He would turn up to lecture at the fair
And do a minor miracle for a fee.
Many a life he whispered up the stair
To teach the black art of anatomy.

He was as deaf to angels as an oak
When, in the fall of Fifteen Ninety-four,
He went to London and crashed through the floor
In mock damnation of the playgoing folk.

Weekending with the scientific crowd,
He met Sir Francis Bacon and helped draft
"Colours of Good and Evil" and read aloud
An obscene sermon at which no one laughed.

He toured the Continent for a hundred years
And subsidized among the peasantry
The puppet play, his tragic history;
With a white glove he boxed the devil's ears
And with a black his own. Tired of this,
He published penny poems about his sins,
In which he placed the heavy emphasis
On the white glove which, for a penny, wins.

Some time before the hemorrhage of the Kings
Of France, he turned respectable and taught;
Quite suddenly everything that he had thought
Seemed to grow scholars' beards and angels' wings.
It was the Overthrow. On Reason's throne
He sat with the fair Phrygian on his knees
And called all universities his own,
As plausible a figure as you please.

Then back to Germany as the sages' sage
To preach comparative science to the young
Who came from every land in a great throng
And knew they heard the master of the age.
When for a secret formula he paid
The Devil another fragment of his soul,
His scholars wept, and several even prayed
That Satan would restore him to them whole.

Backwardly tolerant, Faustus was expelled
From the Third Reich in Nineteen Thirty-nine.
His exit caused the breaching of the Rhine,
Except for which the frontier might have held.
Five years unknown to enemy and friend
He hid, appearing on the sixth to pose
In an American desert at war's end
Where, at his back, a dome of atoms rose.

_{FROM} **Trial of a Poet**

>*Priest.*   What is the character of the crime but
>   madness?

For poets at this hour are demon-ridden,
Pseudo-prophetic and accusatory,
Pseudo-accusatory and very prophetic.
They dabble in forgotten tongues,
They employ the Chaldee and other hieratics,
And emulate the philology of Babel.
Great amateurs of evil, men of the world,
Great friends of the devil and the half-world
They climb down walls to dampness and rot
For a game of barter,
A hair for a sin, a hair for a sin.
And the calm iron-gray honorable poets who dwell in
          towers
Traffic indecently with midwives and mediums
For the old rubbish of lore
Or a chance key or a polluted letter.

Doctor.   Genius is the character of the crime
I have no doubt. Genius must break the law
As Columbus broke the egg.
Genius is man in advance, is therefore mad
Because he pushes darkness over the edge of the world.
We do not like the law broken
Even when the law is palpably absurd,
And even when the law is acknowledged nonsense
We clap genius in irons and send him home to rot;
We pay him with darkness for the light he shed.
That is why genius is with us today.
He did not discover that the world was round
Or that the sun stands still or the blood moves;
All he discovered was a form of verse
That suited and excited the experts in these questions.
Yet it appears he felt it as a crime
Because he fought for his innovation
Like a possessed man, as the Priest puts it.
Out of his new-found phrases and dead footnotes
He wove a critique of life, a bad world history,
With a Cloud-Cuckoo-Land for his heroes
And a hell in minute detail for the rest.
I think we must find the bridge between
This harmless sublimation and his consummate crime.

Israel

When I think of the liberation of Palestine,
When my eye conceives the great black English line
Spanning the world news of two thousand years,
My heart leaps forward like a hungry dog,
My heart is thrown back on its tangled chain,
My soul is hangdog in a Western chair.

When I think of the battle for Zion I hear
The drop of chains, the starting forth of feet
And I remain chained in a Western chair.
My blood beats like a bird against a wall,
I feel the weight of prisons in my skull
Falling away; my forebears stare through stone.

When I see the name of Israel high in print
The fences crumble in my flesh; I sink
Deep in a Western chair and rest my soul.
I look the stranger clear to the blue depths
Of his unclouded eye. I say my name
Aloud for the first time unconsciously.

Speak of the tillage of a million heads
No more. Speak of the evil myth no more
Of one who harried Jesus on his way

Saying, *Go faster*. Speak no more
Of the yellow badge, *secta nefaria*.
Speak the name only of the living land.

Ego

Ego is not persona: in childhood
He rules the little senses, plays at eyes,
Betters the nose, learns warm and soft and cold,
Reacts but cannot act. Ego is old:
He fights but neither laughs nor cries,
Stares but is neither bad nor good.

Ego is not narcissus: if in youth
He lingers at the mirror, he is clear,
Is not in love and never seeks a friend,
Makes all dependent yet does not depend,
Inspects, indulges, does not fear,
Remembers all. Ego is truth.

Ego does not desire or acquire,
Is not the mouth and not the reaching hand,
Dreams never, sleeps at bedtime, rises first,
Sees that the hell of darkness is dispersed,
Is pale in winter, in summer tanned,
Functions alike in ice and fire.

Ego domesticated serves the man
But is no servant, stands aside for will,
Gives no advice, takes none. Ego can fail;

Pampered he softens, struck withdraws like snail.
Trust him to know and to keep still,
Love him as much as brother can.

The Figurehead

Watching my paralytic friend
Caught in the giant clam of himself
Fast on the treacherous shoals of his bed,
I look away to the place he had left
Where at a decade's distance he appeared
To pause in his walk and think of a limp.
One day he arrived at the street bearing
The news that he dragged an ancient foot:
The people on their porches seemed to sway.

Though there are many wired together
In this world and the next, my friend
Strains in his clamps. He is all sprung
And locked in the rust of inner change.
The therapist who plucks him like a harp
Is a cold torture: the animal bleats
And whimpers on its far seashore
As she leans to her find with a smooth hunger.

Somewhere in a storm my pity went down:
It was a wooden figurehead
With sea-hard breasts and polished mouth.
But women wash my friend with brine
From shallow inlets of their eyes,

And women rock my friend with waves
That pulsate from the female moon.
They gather at his very edge and haul
My driftwood friend toward their fires.

Speaking of dancing, joking of sex,
I watch my paralytic friend
And seek my pity in those wastes where he
Becomes my bobbing figurehead.
Then as I take my leave I wade
Loudly into the shallows of his pain,
I splash like a vacationer,
I scare his legs and stir the time of day
With rosy clouds of sediment.

Glass Poem

The afternoon lies glazed upon the wall
And on the window shines the scene-like bay,
And on the dark reflective floor a ray
Falls, and my thoughts like ashes softly fall.

And I look up as one who looks through glass
And sees the thing his soul clearly desires,
Who stares until his vision flags and tires,
But from whose eye the image fails to pass;

Until a wish crashes the vitreous air
And comes to your real hands across this space,

Thief-like and deeply cut to touch your face,
Dearly, most bitterly to touch your hair.

And I could shatter these transparent lights,
Could thrust my arms and bring your body through,
Break from the subtle spectrum the last hue
And change my eyes to dark soft-seeing nights.

But the sun stands and the hours stare like brass
And day flows thickly into permanent time,
And toward your eyes my threatening wishes climb
Where you move through a sea of solid glass.

The Minute

The office building treads the marble dark,
The mother-clock with wide and golden dial
Suffers and glows. Now is the hour of birth
Of the tremulous egg. Now is the time of correction.
O midnight, zero of eternity,
Soon on a million bureaus of the city
Will lie the new-born minute.

The new-born minute on the bureau lies,
Scratching the glass with infant kick, cutting
With diamond cry the crystal and expanse
Of timelessness. This pretty tick of death
Etches its name upon the air. I turn
Titanically in distant sleep, expelling
From my lungs the bitter gas of life.

The loathsome minute grows in length and strength,
Bending its spring to forge an iron hour
That rusts from link to link, the last one bright,
The late one dead. Between the shining works
Range the clean angels, studying that tick
Like a strange dirt, but will not pick it up
Nor move it gingerly out of harm's way.

An angel is stabbed and is carried aloft howling,
For devils have gathered on a ruby jewel
Like red mites on a berry; others arrive
To tend the points with oil and smooth the heat.
See how their vicious faces, lit with sweat,
Worship the train of wheels; see how they pull
The tape-worm Time from nothing into thing.

I with my distant heart lie wide awake
Smiling at that Swiss-perfect engine room
Driven by tiny evils. Knowing no harm
Even of gongs that loom and move in towers
And hands as high as iron masts, I sleep,
At which sad sign the angels in a flock
Rise and sweep past me, spinning threads of fear.

Love for a Hand

Two hands lie still, the hairy and the white,
And soon down ladders of reflected light
The sleepers climb in silence. Gradually
They separate on paths of long ago,

Each winding on his arm the unpleasant clew
That leads, live as a nerve, to memory.

But often when too steep her dream descends,
Perhaps to the grotto where her father bends
To pick her up, the husband wakes as though
He had forgotten something in the house.
Motionless he eyes the room that glows
With the little animals of light that prowl

This way and that. Soft are the beasts of light
But softer still her hand that drifts so white
Upon the whiteness. How like a water-plant
It floats upon the black canal of sleep,
Suspended upward from the distant deep
In pure achievement of its lovely want!

Quietly then he plucks it and it folds
And is again a hand, small as a child's.
He would revive it but it barely stirs
And so he carries it off a little way
And breaks it open gently. Now he can see
The sweetness of the fruit, his hand eats hers.

The Phenomenon

How lovely it was, after the official fright,
To walk in the shadowy drifts, as if the clouds
Saturated with the obscurity of night
Had died and fallen piecemeal into shrouds.

What crepes there were, what sables heaped on stones,
What soft shakos on posts, tragically gay!
And oil-pool flooded fields that blackly shone
The more black under the liquid eye of day!

It was almost warmer to the touch than sands
And sweeter-tasting than the white, and yet
Walking, the children held their fathers' hands
Like visitors to a mine or parapet.

Then black it snowed again and while it fell
You could see the sun, an irritated rim
Wheeling through smoke; each from his shallow hell
Experienced injured vision growing dim.

But one day all was clear, and one day soon,
Sooner than those who witnessed it had died,
Nature herself forgot the phenomenon,
Her faulty snowfall brilliantly denied.

French Postcard

It is so difficult not to go with it
Once it is seen. It tears the mind agape
With butcher force, with intellectual rape,
And the body hangs by a hair above the pit.

In whose brain, when the order was destroyed,
Did it take form and pose, and when the eye
Clicked, was he guillotined into the void
Where the vile emulsion hangs in strips to dry?

It rose with obvious relish to be viewed,
And lay at a sewer's mouth in the grainy dawn
Where a cop found it. It seemed a platitude
Like a bad postcard of the Parthenon.

I know its family tree, its dossier,
Its memory older than Pompeian walls.
Not that it lives but that it looks at day
Shocks. In the night, wherever it is, it calls,

And never fades, but lies flat and uncurled
Even in blast furnace at the fire's core,
Feeding fat tallow to our sunken world
Deep in the riches of our father's drawer.

Going to School

(Phi Beta Kappa poem, Harvard)

What shall I teach in the vivid afternoon
With the sun warming the blackboard and a slip
Of cloud catching my eye?
Only the cones and sections of the moon
Out of some flaking page of scholarship,
Only some foolish heresy
To counteract the authority of prose.
The ink runs freely and the dry chalk flows
Into the silent night of seven slates
Where I create the universe as if
It grew out of some old rabbinic glyph
Or hung upon the necessity of Yeats.

O dry imaginations, drink this dust
That grays the room and powders my coat sleeve,
For in this shaft of light
I dance upon the intellectual crust
Of our own age and hold this make-believe
Like holy-work before your sight.
This is the list of books that time has burned,
These are the lines that only poets have learned,
The frame of dreams, the symbols that dilate;
Yet when I turn from this dark exercise
I meet your bright and world-considering eyes
That build and build and never can create.

I gaze down on the garden with its green
Axial lines and scientific pond
And watch a man in white
Stiffly pursue a butterfly between
Square hedges where he takes it overhand
Into the pocket of his net.
Ah psyche, sinking in the bottled fumes,
Dragging your slow wings while the hunt resumes.
I say, "He placed an image on the pool
Of the Great Mind to float there like a leaf
And then sink downward to the dark belief
Of the Great Memory of the Hermetic School."

I say, "Linnaeus drowned the names of flowers
With the black garlands of his Latin words;
The gardens now are his,
The drug-bright blossoms of the glass are ours.
I think a million taxidermist's birds

Sing in the mind of Agassiz
Who still retained one image of the good,
Who said a fish is but a thought of God.
—This is the flat world circled by its dogs,
This is the right triangle held divine
Before bald Euclid drew his empty line
And shame fell on the ancient astrologues."

The eyes strike angles on the farther wall,
Divine geometry forms upon the page,
I feel a sense of shame.
Then as the great design begins to pall
A cock crows in a laboratory cage
And I proceed. "As for the name,
It is the potency itself of thing,
It is the power-of-rising of the wing;
Without it death and feathers, for neither reed
Of Solomon nor quill of Shakespeare's goose
Ever did more or less than to deduce
Letter from number in our ignorant creed."

And what if he who blessed these walls should walk
Invisibly in the room?—My conscience prates,
"The great biologist
Who read the universe in a piece of chalk
Said all knowledge is good, all learning waits,
And wrong hypotheses exist
To order knowledge and to set it right.
We burn, he said, that others may have light.
These are the penetralia of the school
Of the last century. Under a later sky

We call both saint and fool to prophesy
The second cycle brimming at the full."

Then the clock strikes and I erase the board,
Clearing the cosmos with a sweep of felt,
Voiding my mind as well.
Now that the blank of reason is restored
And they go talking of the crazy Celt
And ghosts that sipped his muscatel,
I must escape their laughter unaware
And sidle past the question on the stair
To gain my office. Is the image lost
That burned and shivered in the speculum
Or does it hover in the upper room?
Have I deceived the student or the ghost?

Here in the quiet of the book-built dark
Where masonry of volumes walls me in
I should expect to find,
Returning to me on a lower arc,
Some image bodying itself a skin,
Some object thinking forth a mind.
This search necessitates no closer look.
I close my desk and choose a modern book
And leave the building. Low, as to astound,
The sun stands with its body on the line
That separates us. Low, as to combine,
The sun touches its image to the ground.

The Alphabet

The letters of the Jews as strict as flames
Or little terrible flowers lean
Stubbornly upwards through the perfect ages,
Singing through solid stone the sacred names.
The letters of the Jews are black and clean
And lie in chain-line over Christian pages.
The chosen letters bristle like barbed wire
That hedge the flesh of man,
Twisting and tightening the book that warns.
These words, this burning bush, this flickering pyre
Unsacrifices the bled son of man
Yet plaits his crown of thorns.

Where go the tipsy idols of the Roman
Past synagogues of patient time,
Where go the sisters of the Gothic rose,
Where go the blue eyes of the Polish women
Past the almost natural crime,
Past the still speaking embers of ghettos,
There rise the tinder flowers of the Jews.
The letters of the Jews are dancing knives
That carve the heart of darkness seven ways.
These are the letters that all men refuse

And will refuse until the king arrives
And will refuse until the death of time
And all is rolled back in the book of days.

The Olive Tree

Save for a lusterless honing-stone of moon
The sky stretches its flawless canopy
Blue as the blue silk of the Jewish flag
Over the valley and out to sea.
It is bluest just above the olive tree.
You cannot find in twisted Italy
So straight a one; it stands not on a crag,
Is not humpbacked with bearing in scored stone,
But perfectly erect in my front yard,
Oblivious of its fame. The fruit is hard,
Multitudinous, acid, tight on the stem;
The leaves ride boat-like in the brimming sun,
Going nowhere and scooping up the light.
It is the silver tree, the holy tree,
Tree of all attributes.
                          Now on the lawn
The olives fall by thousands, and I delight
To shed my tennis shoes and walk on them,
Pressing them coldly into the deep grass,
In love and reverence for the total loss.

The First Time

Behind shut doors, in shadowy quarantine,
There shines the lamp of iodine and rose
That stains all love with its medicinal bloom.
This boy, who is no more than seventeen,
Not knowing what to do, takes off his clothes
As one might in a doctor's anteroom.

Then in a cross-draft of fear and shame
Feels love hysterically burn away,
A candle swimming down to nothingness
Put out by its own wetted gusts of flame,
And he stands smooth as uncarved ivory
Heavily curved for some expert caress.

And finally sees the always open door
That is invisible till the time has come,
And half falls through as through a rotten wall
To where chairs twist with dragons from the floor
And the great bed drugged with its own perfume
Spreads its carnivorous flower-mouth for all.

The girl is sitting with her back to him;
She wears a black thing and she rakes her hair,
Hauling her round face upward like moonrise;
She is younger than he, her angled arms are slim
And like a country girl her feet are bare.
She watches him behind her with old eyes,

Transfixing him in space like some grotesque,
Far, far from her where he is still alone
And being here is more and more untrue.
Then she turns round, as one turns at a desk,
And looks at him, too naked and too soon,
And almost gently asks: *Are you a Jew?*

The Crucifix in the Filing Cabinet

Out of the filing cabinet of true steel
That saves from fire my rags of letters, bills,
Manuscripts, contracts, all the trash of praise
Which one acquires to prove and prove his days;

Out of the drawer that rolls on hidden wheels
I drew a crucifix with beaded chain,
Still new and frightened-looking and absurd.
I picked it up as one picks up a bird

And placed it on my palm. It formed a pile
Like a small mound of stones on which there stands
A tree crazy with age, and on the tree
Some ancient teacher hanging by his hands.

I found a velvet bag sewn by the Jews
For holy shawls and frontlets and soft thongs
That bind the arm at morning for great wrongs
Done in a Pharaoh's time. The crucifix

I dropped down in the darkness of this pouch,
Thought tangled with thought and chain with chain,
Till time untie the dark with greedy look,
Crumble the cross and bleed the leathery vein.

The Murder of Moses

By reason of despair we set forth behind you
And followed the pillar of fire like a doubt,
To hold to belief wanted a sign,
Called the miracle of the staff and the plagues
Natural phenomena.

We questioned the expediency of the march,
Gossiped about you. What was escape
To the fear of going forward and Pharaoh's wheels?
When the chariots mired and the army flooded
Our cry of horror was one with theirs.

You always went alone, a little ahead,
Prophecy disturbed you, you were not a fanatic.
The women said you were meek, the men
Regarded you as a typical leader.
You and your black wife might have been foreigners.

We even discussed your parentage; were you really a Jew?
We remembered how Joseph had made himself a prince,
All of us shared in the recognition
Of his skill of management, sense of propriety,
Devotion to his brothers and Israel.

We hated you daily. Our children died. The water
     spilled.
It was as if you were trying to lose us one by one.
Our wandering seemed the wandering of your mind,
The cloud believed we were tireless,
We expressed our contempt and our boredom openly.

At last you ascended the rock; at last returned.
Your anger that day was probably His.
When we saw you come down from the mountain, your
     skin alight
And the stones of our law flashing,
We fled like animals and the dancers scattered.

We watched where you overturned the calf on the fire,
We hid when you broke the tablets on the rock,
We wept when we drank the mixture of gold and water.
We had hoped you were lost or had left us.
This was the day of our greatest defilement.

You were simple of heart; you were sorry for Miriam,
You reasoned with Aaron, who was your enemy.
However often you cheered us with songs and prayers
We cursed you again. The serpent bit us,
And mouth to mouth you entreated the Lord for
     our sake.

At the end of it all we gave you the gift of death.
Invasion and generalship were spared you.
The hand of our direction, resignedly you fell,
And while officers prepared for the river-crossing
The Old God blessed you and covered you with earth.

Though you were mortal and once committed murder
You assumed the burden of the covenant,
Spoke for the world and for our understanding.
Converse with God made you a thinker,
Taught us all early justice, made us a race.

The Bourgeois Poet

The bourgeois poet closes the door of his study and
lights his pipe. Why am I in this box, he says to
himself (although it is exactly as he planned). The
bourgeois poet sits down at his inoffensive desk—
a door with legs, a door turned table—and almost
approves the careful disarray of books, papers,
magazines and such artifacts as thumbtacks. The
bourgeois poet is already out of matches and gets
up. It is too early in the morning for any definite
emotion and the B.P. smokes. It is beautiful in the
midlands: green fields and tawny fields, sorghum
the color of red morocco bindings, distant new
neighborhoods, cleanly and treeless, and the Vet-
erans Hospital fronted with a shimmering Indian
Summer tree. The Beep feels seasonal, placid as a
melon, neat as a child's football lying under the
tree, waiting for whose hands to pick it up.

Sub-Division

Orchards hang in the newspaper of sky. It's snowing
names and addresses over the world, O lovely
splash!

In dry percussion, hammers of prosperity practice
against the too-green corn. The wheat field nar-
rows, then disappears, leaving a memory of dry
wind-waves. Who eats dry wheat but boys, wheat
the hue of the backs of eighteenth-century books.
Children spring from the doors where there are
no trees. Roofer up there, it's been a good day.

On the oldest plains rise the newest houses, smelling of
rose sawdust and nails. The clammy mortar struc-
tures itself. Everyone looks like a possible Sur-
vivor. Is he one? Is she one? Who reinvented the
secret stairway, passage to the room of Poe,
chapel without a god?

Christ is in voice. The mayor is pleased with the murals.
The Jews next door are less noisy. Set the alarm
for seven.

Garrison State

Of love and death in the Garrison State I sing. From uni-
formed populations rises the High Art, *Oedipus
King*, the Nō, the ballerina bleeding in her slip-
pers. At the Officer's Club adultery is rationed
(their children are not allowed to play with guns;
this helps whet their appetite). The ladies are dis-
cussing the chemical control of behavior by radio
waves: that will solve the problem of neighbors.
Symposia on causes of desertion draw record-

breaking crowds. The handsomer pacifists are invited to the most sought-after cocktail parties. The women try their hand at them in the rumpus room; some progress reported. Waves of asceticism sweep the automobile industry. The mere sight of a Sam Browne belt, which used to inspire contempt, brings tears to the eyes of high-school boys. All flabby citizens are automatically put under surveillance. Chess problems supersede crap in the noncoms' barracks. The sacred number is Two: two parties, two powers sworn to mutual death, two poles of everything from ethics to magnetics. It's a balanced society.

Today the order goes out: all distant places are to be abolished: beach-combers are shot like looters. Established poets are forced to wear beards and bluejeans; they are treated kindly in bohemian zoos; mysterious stipends drift their way. They can trade soap for peyote at specified libraries. Children's prizes are given for essays on the pleasures of crisis. Historians are awarded all the key posts in the foreign office. Sculptors who use old shrapnel are made the heads of schools of design. Highways move underground like veins of ore. The Anti-Sky Association (volunteer contributions only) meets naked at high noon and prays for color blindness.

"Color is a biological luxury."

Office Love

Office love, love of money and fight, love of calculated
sex. The offices reek with thin volcanic metal.
Tears fall in typewriters like drops of solder.
Brimstone of brassieres, low voices, the whirr of
dead-serious play. From the tropical tree and the
Rothko in the Board Room to the ungrammatical
broom closet fragrant with waxes, to the vast
typing pool where coffee is being served by dainty
waitresses maneuvering their hand trucks, music
almost unnoticeable falls. The very telephones
are hard and kissable, the electric water cooler
sweetly sweats. Gold simmers to a boil in
braceleted and sunburned cheeks. What ritual
politeness nevertheless, what subtlety of clothing.
And if glances meet, if shoulders graze, there's no
harm done. Flowers, celebrations, pregnancy
leave, how the little diamonds sparkle under the
psychologically soft-colored ceilings. It's an ele-
gant windowless world of soft pressures and effi-
ciency joys, of civilized mishaps—mere runs in
the stocking, papercuts.

Where the big boys sit the language is rougher. Phone
calls to China and a private shower. No paper
visible anywhere. Policy is decided by word of
mouth like gangsters. There the power lies and is
sexless.

High School

Waiting in front of the columnar high school (the old
   ones look like banks, or rather insurance compa-
   nies) I glance over the top of my book. The bells
   go off like slow burglar alarms; innumerable six-
   teeners saunter out. There's no running as in the
   lower schools, none of that helpless gaiety of the
   small. Here comes a surly defiance. As in a ritual,
   each lights a cigaret just at the boundary where
   the tabu ends. Each chews. The ones in cars rev
   up their motors and have bad complexions like
   gangsters. The sixteeners are all playing gangster.

The sea of subjectivity comes at you like a tidal wave,
   splashing the cuffs of middle-aged monuments.
   War is written on their unwritten faces. They try
   out wet dreams and wandering mind. They're
   rubbing Aladdin's lamp in the locker room. They
   pray for moments of objectivity as drunkards pray
   for the one that puts you out. They've captured
   the telephone centers, the microphones, the mag-
   azine syndicates (they've left the movies to us). I
   wait behind the wheel and spy; it's enemy terri-
   tory all right. My daughter comes, grows taller as
   she approaches. It's a moment of panic.

But once at night in the sweet and sour fall I dropped her
   off at the football game. The bowl of light lit up
   the creamy Corinthian columns. A cheer went up
   from the field so shrill, so young, like a thousand

birds in a single cage, like a massacre of child-brides in a clearing, I felt ashamed and grave. The horror of their years stoned me to death.

The Dermatologist

The dermatologist committed suicide, a good man, a sad man, with the hangdog mien of a proctologist.

Skin-watching, tricksy as palmistry, what medieval blips and scars, what outcroppings of thought! Maps of remorse, tattoos from voyages never undertaken, blueprints of literary cleverness, bad dreams of personal acid—the skin has wiles undreamed of by bacteria. Under the living continent of skin flows molten lava; heat spots and sinkings form, then violent eruption, appearance of crystals, the terrifying symmetry of disease. Thus the humiliation of itch- and scratch-lust, tearing of pleasure into pain, revenge of self and desecration of love.

So lay the mother of grown children, after the final consent to herself that the marriage was ended. The dermatologist pronounces the name of the rare sickness. She will lose her skin from top to toe, fingernails, toenails. Yet she will be like new, without a scar, made perfect after agony.

Absences

The two-year-old has had a motherless week. Mother has gone to bring back the baby. A week is many many years. One evening they bring the news to the playpen: a child is born, you have a baby brother. The dark little eyes consider this news and convey no message. One day long after, they arrive in a taxi, father, mother, bundle. The two-year-old observes from her blue walker on the sunny sidewalk. She stares and turns away on her wheels.

The father has gone to the other side of the world. He will bring back strange presents to a strange house. The little ones shyly wait their turn. Reconciliation is gradual.

In Trenton, New Jersey, the soldiers sit in the innocuous bar. It's three years since they saw the ones they wrote to. They are all afraid to go home. One lives two blocks away; he is very silent. Late in the afternoon, at an ungiven signal, they get up and disperse, like criminals perfectly trained for the job ahead.

In my brother's house when I left (whole histories ago) the furniture was honeymoon fresh, gleam of ceramics; soft beige carpets smelt like new-mown hay. With a shock I see the carpet is worn; the sofa has settled; books have changed places. A thousand days of words have passed.

Time is mostly absences, oceans generally at peace, and
lives we love most often out of reach.

Third Class, *Queen Mary*

Third Class, *Queen Mary*, late December on the high
Atlantic. The storm is fabulous. Seas run to the
height of the promenade deck where picture win-
dows are smashed. The ocean frowns like ele-
phant hide and has a texture almost smooth. In
the dining room I am sat with Miss Cohen at a
table for two. (The English keep races together.)
I tell her proudly that this was my troopship.
Proudly I describe the Mary in wartime: gray
from stem to stern, all ports and windows
blacked, the monster zigzagging from Boston to
the Sydney Heads. Forty days and forty nights,
Key West, Rio, Capetown, south almost to Little
America, north to New South Wales. Now it
seems quiet and empty, clean and well-kept as a
cemetery, even in this great storm.—Ah, this is
different, says Miss Cohen: we are paying for this.

We are paying for this!

The server is polite and clean. He tends us in the mighty
empty ship. The tablecloth is white, the silver
silver. The waiters call me Sir. This voyage I am
Sir. I pay.

In the vulgarity of poetic justice, Miss Cohen is knocked
from her chair by a skyscraper sea. I visit her in
the hospital. She is ugly; I like her. I say to myself,
she offended the god of the storm.

Tahiti 1936

The poet takes the voyage to the New Cytherea. Fifty
miles from little Papeete he and his girl have
rented a thatched hut. He says the name of the
district over and over: Taravao, Taravao. The hut
is right on the beach; water laps at the pilings.
The whole front opens crazily out and is propped
up by a stake. The roof is pandanus, very brown
and dusty, a house of straw. No sooner have they
entered when the poet grabs up a witch's broom
and begins to sweep. The girl hangs batiks on the
wall. There are spiders big as your hand. Frozen
with terror the poet smashes them.

Over the water rises Moorea, blue-mauve with lots of
red, as the painter saw it. The poet sweeps and
arranges like a woman. He lays out books. The
hut is ready at last; they lean out of the open wall
and worship the world. They make love on the
crunchy bed. Later the natives bring bananas as a
gift. Their movements are slow and peaceful,
their French is soft and broad. Inside the coral

reef the swimming is perfect. They shop in Pa-
peete. They bank at the Bank of Indo-China.
Everything is exotic, even the nuns. At the Post
Office a crowd of French sailors are arguing
grimly. Spain is at war with itself. It has started
today. It is even here.

There is only one movie: *Tabu* by Murnau. The natives
return to it like a church. We go there. It is great
like literature.

Burlesk

Hart Crane, though handicapped, did well with the
burlesk: all but her belly buried in the floor. Mag-
dalene? Perhaps. In Kansas City I pay my respects
to the dying art. The theater is in ruins, the
ticket-taker only half-conscious. Wine took him
long ago. The carpet in the aisle is ripped; twice I
snag my foot. The rank air smells of disinfectant.
All seats are vacant except the first two rows.
These are lit up as in a Rembrandt picture, the
glowing center of the operation. I sit down inches
from the drum. It lifts my hair each second it is
smashed. The snare drum hisses and the block
clicks. The cymbal crazes.

She's halfway through, already down to the sash that
hangs like a silk muffler between her buttocks.

She gyrates with an expert beat, more round than sharp. Small-breasted, her nipples glitter with stardust—some local ordinance. She is very pretty, not what you would expect, almost indifferently dancing her career. Cold flows from her steady limbs; stately she spreads her thighs for the climactic grind, when at the highest throw she slips her final string, holding one hand over the part like a live fig leaf, and flittering her fingers off—and we are there, and she is all but hairless.

Our faces light up with intelligence.

Bouquet

All tropic places smell of mold. A letter from Karachi smells of mold. A book I had in New Guinea twenty years ago smells of mold. Cities in India smell of mold and dung. After a while you begin to like it. The curry dishes in the fine Bombay restaurant add the dung flavor. In the villages dung patties plastered to the walls, the leaving of the cows the only cooking fuel. The smell rubs into the blood.

Paris in the winter smells of wood smoke and fruit. Near the Gare St. Lazare in the freezing dusk the crowds pour slowly down the streets in every direction. A police van the size of a Pullman car goes at a walking pace. The gendarme keeps jumping down from the rear like a streetcar conductor in the old days. He is examining identity cards of pedestrians, especially the females. A girl comes swinging along, her pocketbook in rhythm with her behind. She is bareheaded and wears a raincoat. The gendarme examines her identity card. She is motioned into the paddy wagon.

Salzburg, the castle smells of snow and peat. Baltimore, old oaken bucket. Portsmouth, Virginia, roses and diesel oil. Dublin, coal dust, saccharine whiskey, bitter bodies. Damp gusts of Siena doorways. Warehouses of Papeete, acrid smell of copra, frangipani, salt water and mold. Smell of rotting water in Hollandia.

Unbreathable jungles, parks subtle and cool. Backstage the ballet dancers wipe their sweat; "the entire stage stinks like a stable." Sewer gas of beauty parlors. Electric smell of hair in rut. Talcum powder, earliest recollection. Rome, the armpit of the universe.

War Movies

I wait up for the movies of my war, late, late at night on television. It comes with crackling fanfare, with faulty memory for the facts of life. But it's true enough to keep me awake, staring in the dark, groping my way back to my war. It's true, not true to life. I study the hair of the sweethearts that hangs to their shoulders (yours was like that), the square-shouldered dresses, junk jewelry and all. Farewells, convoys, dawn bombardments, palm trees nestling Japs in their crotches. I hear the faded propaganda message on the dying lips of the handsome actor; my heart pounds to the pull of the flag in the artificial wind. And the next assault, and the next. And the homecoming. Homecoming destroys me: I weep. (I'm glad you are asleep.)

Those movies under the moon in New Guinea, helmets clanking quietly in the mud as we watched the giantess dancing our heartbreak. Movies shut off while the air raid passed, rot of coconuts, our own bad sweat asserting itself till the dream returned. Movies of the moving thigh and the honey-thick ballad heavy as ether. Mistaken-identity movies, pie-throwing movies, no movies of war in the war zone. These are saved for my middle-aged bed.

Fox Hole

Quintana lay in the shallow grave of coral. The guns boomed stupidly fifty yards away. The plasma trickled into his arm. Naked and filthy, covered with mosquitoes, he looked at me as I read his

white cloth tag. How do you feel, Quintana? He
looks away from my gaze. I lie: we'll get you out
of here sometime today.

I never saw him again, dead or alive. Skin and bones,
with eyes as soft as soot, neck long as a thigh, a
cross on his breastbone not far from the dog tags.
El Greco was all I could think of. Quintana lying
in his shallow foxhole waiting to be evacuated. A
dying man with a Spanish name equals El Greco.
A truck driver from Dallas probably.

When the Japs were making the banzai charge, to add
insult to death, they came at us screaming the
supreme insult: *Babe Ruth, go to hell!* The Ameri-
cans, on the other hand, when the Japs flew over
dropping sticks of explosives, shouted into the air,
as if they could hear: *Tojo, eat shit!*

Soldiers fall in love with the enemy all too easily. It's the
allies they hate. Every war is its own excuse.
That's why they're all surrounded with ideals.
That's why they're all crusades.

The Missal

Priests and Freudians will understand. In the throttling
Papuan heat, even the rain is hot, even the rain
carries the rot smell. Lying in mud or in soaked

hammocks the soldiers stew and joke and empty their dead minds. Deprived of love and letters and the sight of woman, the dead mind rots.

Who sent this missal soft and black, with iridescent gold and five silk ribbons sewn in the binding: red, silver, blue, green, purple? Two thousand pages mica-thin, like two millennia of daily shame.

Nearby, the natives make themselves strong by drinking sweat of warriors, eating fingernails coated with human blood. Priests and Freudians comprehend. And now I learn the missal prayers. I set up mental prayer wheels and spin them with the whips of fear. Help me, Freudians and priests: when I say the proud Hail Mary, the serpent takes me in the groin.

I seek the chaplain in his tent. Father, convert me. He looks at me and says: You must excuse me, sergeant. I have a furlough coming up.

When I say the Hail Mary I get an erection. Doesn't that prove the existence of God?

I Am an Atheist Who Says His Prayers

I am an atheist who says his prayers.

I am an anarchist, and a full professor at that. I take the loyalty oath.

I am a deviate. I fondle and contribute, backscuttle and brown, father of three.

I stand high in the community. My name is in *Who's Who*. People argue about my modesty.

I drink my share and yours and never have enough. I free-load officially and unofficially.

A physical coward, I take on all intellectuals, established poets, popes, rabbis, chiefs of staff.

I am a mystic. I will take an oath that I have seen the Virgin. Under the dry pandanus, to the scratching of kangaroo rats, I achieve psychic onanism. My tree of nerves electrocutes itself.

I uphold the image of America and force my luck. I write my own ticket to oblivion.

I am of the race wrecked by success. The audience brings me news of my death. I write out of boredom, despise solemnity. The wrong reason is good enough for me.

I am of the race of the prematurely desperate. In poverty of comfort I lay gunpowder plots. I lapse my insurance.

I am the Babbitt metal of the future. I never read more than half of a book. But that half I read forever.

I love the palimpsest, statues without heads, fertility dolls
     of the continent of Mu. I dream prehistory, the
     invention of dye. The palms of the dancers' hands
     are vermillion. Their heads oscillate like the co-
     bra. High-caste woman smelling of earth and silk,
     you can dry my feet with your hair.

I take my place beside the Philistine and unfold my nap-
     kin. This afternoon I defend the Marines. I gog-
     gle at long cars.

Without compassion I attack the insane. Give them the
     horsewhip!

The homosexual lectures me brilliantly in the beer
     booth. I can feel my muscles soften. He smiles at
     my terror.

Pitchpots flicker in the lemon groves. I gaze down on
     the plains of Hollywood. My fine tan and my
     arrogance, my gray hair and my sneakers, O
     Israel!

Wherever I am I become. The power of entry is with me.
     In the doctor's office a patient, calm and humili-
     ated. In the foreign movies a native, shabby
     enough. In the art gallery a person of authority
     (there's a secret way of approaching a picture.
     Others move off). The high official insults me to
     my face. I say nothing and accept the job. He of-
     fers me whiskey.

How beautifully I fake! I convince myself with men's
    room jokes and epigrams. I paint myself into a
    corner and escape on pulleys of the unknown.
    Whatever I think at the moment is true. Turn me
    around in my tracks; I will take your side.

For the rest, I improvise and am not spiteful and water
    the plants on the cocktail table.

Lower the Standard

Lower the standard: that's my motto. Somebody is al-
    ways putting the food out of reach. We're tired of
    falling off ladders. Who says a child can't paint? A
    pro is somebody who does it for money. Lower
    the standards. Let's all play poetry. Down with
    ideals, flags, convention buttons, morals, the
    scrambled eggs on the admiral's hat. I'm talking
    sense. Lower the standards. Sabotage the stylistic
    approach. Let weeds grow in the subdivision.
    Putty up the incisions in the library façade, those
    names that frighten grade-school teachers, those
    names whose U's are cut like V's. Burn the *Syn-
    topicon* and *The Harvard Classics*. Lower the stan-
    dard on classics, battleships, Russian ballet, na-
    tional anthems (but they're low enough). Break
    through to the bottom. Be natural as an Ameri-
    can abroad who knows no language, not even
    American. Keelhaul the poets in the vestry chairs.

Renovate the Abbey of cold-storage dreamers. Get off the Culture Wagon. Learn how to walk the way you want. Slump your shoulders, stick your belly out, arms all over the table. How many generations will this take? Don't think about it, just make a start. (You have made a start.) Don't break anything you can step around, *but don't pick it up*. The law of gravity is the law of art. You first, poetry second, the good, the beautiful, the true come last. As the lad said: We must love one another or die.

Prosody

Why am I happy writing this textbook? What sublime idiocy! What a waste of time! A textbook on prosody at that. Yet when I sit down to comb the business out, when I address the easel of this task, I burn with an even flame, I'm cooking with gas. There are some things so dull they hypnotize like the pendulum of a clock; so clockwork and quotidian they make the flesh delirious like fresh water. X-ray the poem, give it a thorough physical, a clean bill of health. We can see everything but the flow of blood. What Latin and Greek nomenclature! But this is order, order made to order. This is system to plot and plan. This is definition, edges clean as razors. Simplification, boldface, indented. I know there is no such thing as a textbook.

I know that all textbooks are sold the second the course is over. I know that a book sold is a dead book. And I dream, like others, of writing a textbook that is not a textbook, a book that not even a student would part with, a book that makes even prosody breathe. So, when the sun shines with the nine o'clock brightness and the coffee swims in my throat and the smoke floats over the page like the smoke of a ship's funnel, then I romanticize. I make a muse of prosody, old hag. She's just a registered nurse, I know, I know, but I have her sashay, grind and bump, register Alcaics, Sapphics, choriambs (my predilection). She's trained all right. She's second nature herself. She knows her job, I mine. We'll work it out: it may be poetry. Blueprints are blue. They have their dreams.

The Funeral of Poetry

The password of the twentieth century: Communications (as if we had to invent them). Animals and cannibals have communications; birds and bees and even a few human creatures called artists (generally held to be insane). But the bulk of humanity had to invent Communications. The Romans had the best roads in the world, but had nothing to communicate over them except other Romans. Americans have conquered world-time and world-space and chat with the four corners of the earth at breakfast. The entire solar system is in the hands of cartoonists.

I am sitting in the kitchen in Nebraska and watching a shrouded woman amble down the market in Karachi. She is going to get her morning small-pox shot. It's cold and mental love they want. It's the mystic sexuality of Communications. The girl hugs the hi-fi speaker to her belly: it pours into her openings like gravy. Money was love. Power was love. Communications now are love. In the spring Hitler arises. This is the time of trampling.

A man appears at the corner of the street; I prepare my-self for hospitality. Man or angel, welcome! But I am afraid and double-lock the door. On the occa-sion of the death of a political party, I send an epitaph by Western Union. I didn't go to the fu-neral of poetry. I stayed home and watched it on television.

Manhole Covers

The beauty of manhole covers—what of that?
Like medals struck by a great savage khan,
Like Mayan calendar stones, unliftable, indecipherable,
Not like the old electrum, chased and scored,
Mottoed and sculptured to a turn,
But notched and whelked and pocked and smashed
With the great company names
(Gentle Bethlehem, smiling United States).
This rustproof artifact of my street,
Long after roads are melted away will lie
Sidewise in the grave of the iron-old world,
Bitten at the edges,
Strong with its cryptic American,
Its dated beauty.

Western Town

Strange western town at the round edge of night,
Into your sleep the broad-shouldered train
Gentles its way, absorbed in its thunderous quiet,
Shearing off porches of carpenter's gothic,
Gathering bulbs and crocuses of electricity.

Now the green blinds of country stores go down
And arches of gold lettering gleam
Like old asbestos in dead movie houses.

Heart-heavy in the cool compartments
The traveling men turn over in their sleep
As the pale squares of light, newspaper thin,
Fall on their eyelids again and again and again,
Plunging the sleepers into a deeper sleep,
A deeper drift of linen than their dream.

Perhaps a single figure is let down
In the hometown dark, or maybe not;
Perhaps only the sleepy sacks of mail
Or a lone coffin come by rail
At rest now on a sketchy cart. Tomorrow,
Somewhere the city will take the train apart.

New Museum

Entering the new museum we feel first
The rubbery values of a doctor's walls,
Cinnamon, buff, gunmetal, rose of gray,
But these almost immediately fade away,
Leaving the windowless white light
That settles only on the works of art—
A far cry from the stained cathedrals where
Masterpieces crack in the bad air
Of candle grease, conversation, and prayer,
Ours is the perfect viewing atmosphere.

Walking around, we are much quieter here
Than in the great basilicas,
The great basilicas of Christendom.
Those freezing niches were the masters' home;
Our galleries warm us like a hotel room
Of cinnamon, powder blue, eggshell of rose,
And yet our painters paint as from a bruise,
The blues neither transparent nor opaque,
The blacks so dry they seem a dust of black.
These are the patterns which our feelings make.

They paint their images as if through smoke,
With now and then a falling coal of red
And now and then a yellow burst, like shock;
They paint the damaged tissue magnified,
The lower land, the structure of the thing;
They paint the darkened luminous optic lake
Through which our eyes, though blind,
See all the lines of force and points of stress
In the scientific field of dark.
These are the patterns which our feelings make.

There is such light in darkness that we see
Blueprints of dreams, child's play, prehistory,
And caves and Altamiras of the mind;
These painters kiss with open eyes to make
Miles of Picassos and the double nose.
Soothed by the blues and blacks, our eyes unclose
To drink great gulps of darkness in;
O skies that fall away time after time
Where tracers of emotion miss the mark
But leave the patterns which our feelings make!

These images have all come home like crows
That cross the hot wheat of the last van Goghs
And cross everything out;
His sorrow saw the thick-skinned peeling sun
Explode above the terrified sunflowers.
Our painters stumble through his private night,
Follow the weak shout of the electric light
Deeper into the caves and offices
Where doctors hang abstractions, blue and black.
These are the patterns which our feelings make.

The Poetry Reading

He takes the lectern in his hands
And, like a pilot at his instruments,
Checks the position of his books, the time,
The glass of water, and the slant of light;
Then, leaning forward on guy-wire nerves,
He elevates the angle of his nose
And powers his soul into the evening.

Now, if ever, he must begin to climb
To that established height
Where one hypnotically remains aloft,
But at the thought, as if an engine coughed,
He drops, barely clearing the first three rows,
Then quakes, recovers, and upward swerves,
And hangs there on his perilous turning fans.

O for more altitude, to spin a cloud
Of crystals, as the cloud writes poetry
In nature's wintry sport!
Or for that hundred-engined voice of wings
That, rising with a turtle in its claws,
Speeds to a rock and drops it heavily,
Where it bursts open with a loud report!

Or for that parchment voice of wrinkled vowels,
That voice of all the ages, polyglot,
Sailing death's boat
Past fallen towers of foreign tours—
The shrouded voice troubled with stony texts,
Voice of all souls and of sacred owls,
Darkly intoning from the tailored coat!

Or for the voice of order, witty and good,
Civilizing the ears of the young and rude,
Weaving the music of ideas and forms,
Writing encyclopedias of hope.
Or for that ever higher voice that swarms
Like a bright monkey up religion's rope
To all those vacant thrones.

But he who reads thinks as he drones his song:
What do they think, those furrows of faces,
Of a poet of the middle classes?
Is he a poet at all? His face is fat.
Can the anthologies have his birthday wrong?
He looks more like an aging bureaucrat
Or a haberdasher than a poet of eminence.

He looks more like a Poet-in-Residence

O to be *declassé*, or low, or high,
Criminal, bastard, or aristocrat—
Anything but the norm, the in-between!
Oh, martyr him for his particular vice,
Make him conspicuous at any price,
Save him, O God, from being nice.

Whom the gods love die young. Too late for that,
Too late also to find a different job,
He is condemned to fly from room to room
And, like a parakeet, be beautiful,
Or, like a grasshopper in a grammar school,
Leap for the window that he'll never find,
And take off with a throb and come down blind.

Tornado Warning

It is a beauteous morning but the air turns sick,
The April freshness seems to rot, a curious smell.
Above the wool-pack clouds a rumor stains the sky,
A fallow color deadening atmosphere and mind.
The air gasps horribly for breath, sucking itself
In spasms of sharp pain, light drifts away.
Women walk on grass, a few husbands come home,
Bushes and trees stop dead, children gesticulate,
Radios warn to open windows, tell where to hide.

The pocky cloud mammato-cumulus comes on,
Downward-projecting bosses of brown cloud grow
Lumps on lymphatic sky, blains, tumors, and dugs,
Heavy cloud-boils that writhe in general disease of sky,
While bits of hail clip at the crocuses and clunk
At cars and windowglass.

      We cannot see the mouth,
We cannot see the mammoth's neck hanging from
  cloud,
Snout open, lumbering down ancient Nebraska
Where dinosaur lay down in deeps of clay and died,
And towering elephant fell and billion buffalo.
We cannot see the horror-movie of the funnel-cloud
Snuffing up cows, crazing the cringing villages,
Exploding homes and barns, bursting the level lakes.

Human Nature

For months and years in a forgotten war
I rode the battle-gray Diesel-stinking ships
Among the brilliantly advertised Pacific Islands,
Coasting the sinister New Guinea Coasts,
All during the killing and hating of a forgotten war.
Now when I drive behind a Diesel-stinking bus
On the way to the university to teach
Stevens and Pound and Mallarmé,
I am homesick for war.

California Winter

It is winter in California, and outside
Is like the interior of a florist shop:
A chilled and moisture-laden crop
Of pink camellias lines the path; and what
Rare roses for a banquet or a bride,
So multitudinous that they seem a glut!

A line of snails crosses the golf-green lawn
From the rosebushes to the ivy bed;
An arsenic compound is distributed
For them. The gardener will rake up the shells
And leave in a corner of the patio
The little mound of empty snails, like skulls.

By noon the fog is burnt off by the sun
And the world's immensest sky opens a page
For the exercises of a future age;
Now jet planes draw straight lines, parabolas,
And x's, which the wind, before they're done,
Erases leisurely or pulls to fuzz.

It is winter in the valley of the vine.
The vineyards crucified on stakes suggest
War cemeteries, but the fruit is pressed,
The redwood vats are brimming in the shed,
And on the sidings stand tank cars of wine,
For which bright juice a billion grapes have bled.

And skiers from the snow line driving home
Descend through almond orchards, olive farms,
Fig tree and palm tree—everything that warms
The imagination of the wintertime.
If the walls were older one would think of Rome:
If the land were stonier one would think of Spain.

But this land grows the oldest living things,
Trees that were young when Pharaohs ruled the world,
Trees whose new leaves are only just unfurled.
Beautiful they are not; they oppress the heart
With gigantism and with immortal wings;
And yet one feels the sumptuousness of this dirt.

It is raining in California, a straight rain
Cleaning the heavy oranges on the bough,
Filling the gardens till the gardens flow,
Shining the olives, tiling the gleaming tile,
Waxing the dark camellia leaves more green,
Flooding the daylong valleys like the Nile.

You Played Chopin

You played Chopin at ten at my request,
Ten in the morning while I opened beer,
Myself a somewhat uninvited guest,
Yourself lost in the melody, lost in fear.
The heavy nocturne like old damask hung
In the half-empty house while your young child
Wandered half-lost between us and among
Tables and chairs . . . myself silent and wild,
Yourself proud and resentful. Then you said
Read one of your poems, and brought the book.
Wasn't it Baudelaire's *Giantess* I read
That I'd translated on a troopship? Look,
Eleven months have passed and the birds sing
Since that strange morning that changed everything.

How Do I Love You?

How do I love you? I don't even know
Now we're cut off again like a bad phone
(Faulty communications are my middle name).
Everything is the same and not the same,
You are still here but also you are gone
And soon I shall be far away also.
How does it matter that I wish you well,

That no one weaken your resolve to go?
How do I love you? Is it just a game
To love your sadness and possess your name?
And now you have no reason to be sad
Do I lose the little of you that I had?
And if I've lost you who is there to blame?
(Faulty communications are my middle name).

You Lay Above Me

You lay above me on that beautiful day,
Your dark eyes made more dark with tiny wings
You drew to prick my kisses with beestings.
Your russet hair in heavy brushstrokes lay
Against the pastel of the Nebraska sky
And all around the stippled poplar trees
Framed you like an unpainted masterpiece.
Some birds spoke out and airplanes coming over,
And now and then a farmer peered our way
Where we were stretched out on the new green grass
On a green blanket, to see a white-haired lover
And a wine-colored, flower-printed creature,
As mythologically dark and dazzling as
The sun that forces frozen earth to nature.

O My Beloved

O my beloved and the days go by
And we can't tell which day or week or why
Because what does it matter when I have
The long-eyed Renoir *enfant* that you gave,

Knowing it has your sweet ambiguous eyes
Which now I kiss, your hands that tantalize,
Your breasts that open to me and your thighs,
Your arms that lift up music from the keys,
Your shadowy voice with all its harmonies,
The words you write and those we read together,
The wine you take into your perfect lips
From mine, your tongue made musky by those grapes,
Your look of parting like a darkening sky,
Your wave as sovereign as a peacock feather.

Aubade

Et c'est la fin pour quoy sommes ensemble.

What dawn is it?

The morning star stands at the end of your street as you watch me turn to laugh a kind of goodbye, with love-crazed head like a white satyr moving through wet bushes.

The morning star bursts in my eye like a hemorrhage as I enter my car in a dream surrounded by your heavenly-earthly smell.

The steering wheel is sticky with dew,

The golf course is empty, husbands stir in their sleep desiring, and though no cocks crow in suburbia, the birds are making a hell of a racket.

Into the newspaper dawn as sweet as your arms that hold the old new world, dawn of green lights that smear the empty streets with come and go.

It is always dawn when I say goodnight to you,
Dawn of wrecked hair and devastated beds,
Dawn when protective blackness turns to blue and lovers
    drive sunward with peripheral vision.
—To improvise a little on Villon,
Dawn is the end for which we are together.
My house of loaded ashtrays and unwashed glasses, tulip
    petals and columbine that spill on the table and splash
    on the floor,
My house full of your dawns,
My house where your absence is presence,
My slum that loves you, my bedroom of dustmice and
    cobwebs, of local paintings and eclectic posters, my
    bedroom of rust neckties and divorced mattresses, and
    of two of your postcards, *Pierrot with Flowers* and *Young
    Girl with Cat*,
My bed where you have thrown your body down like a
    king's ransom or a boa constrictor.
But I forgot to say: May passed away last night,
May died in her sleep.
That May that blessed and kept our love in fields and
    motels.
I erect a priapic statue to that May for lovers to kiss as long
    as I'm in print, and polish as smooth as the Pope's toe.
This morning came June of spirea and platitudes,
This morning came June discreetly dressed in gray,
June of terrific promises and lawsuits.
And where are the poems that got lost in the shuffle of
    spring?
Where is the poem about the eleventh of March, when
    we raised the battleflag of dawn?

Where is the poem about the coral necklace that
   whipped your naked breasts in leaps of love?
The poem concerning the ancient lover we followed
   through your beautiful sleeping head?
The fire-fountain of your earthquake thighs and your
   electric mouth?
Where is the poem about the little one who says my
   name and watches us almost kissing in the sun?
The vellum stretchmarks on your learned belly,
Your rosy-fingered nightgown of nylon and popcorn,
Your razor that caresses your calves like my hands?
Where are the poems that are already obsolete, leaves of
   last month, a very historical month?
Maybe I'll write them, maybe I won't, no matter,
And this is the end for which we are together.
Et c'est la fin pour quoy sommes ensemble.

Adult Bookstore

Round the green fountain thick with women
Abstract in the concrete, water trickling
Between their breasts, wetting their waists
Girdled with wheat, pooling in the basin,
The walker pauses, shrugs, peregrinates
To the intersection, section of the city
Where forgotten fountains struggle for existence,
Shops have declined to secondhand
And marginal cultures collect like algae.
Dubious enterprises flourish here,
The massage parlor, the adult bookstore.

Their windows are either yellowed or blacked
Or whited or redded out,
Bold lettering proclaiming No Minors Allowed,
Bachelor Books, Adult Films and Cartoons.

The doorway jogs to the right at a strict angle
And everything from the street is invisible,
Keeping the law and clutching the illusion.
Inside, the light is cold and clean and bright,
Everything sanitary, wrapped in cellophane

Which flashes messages from wall to wall
Of certain interest to the eye that reads

Or does not read: Randy, Coit,
Sex Hold-Up, Discipline, Ghetto Male,
Images of cruelty, ideas for the meek,
Scholarly peeks at French, English and Greek,
And everywhere the more than naked nude
Mystery called the wound that never heals.

Or there a surgical cabinet all glass:
Pink plastic phalli, prickly artifact,
Enlarger finger-small or stallion-size,
Inflatable love partner, five feet four.
Lotions, Hot Melt, super-double-dong,
Battery dildo (origin obscure),
Awakeners of the tired heart's desire
When love goes wrong.

The expense of spirit in a waste of shame
Is sold forever to the single stag
Who takes it home in a brown paper bag.

Girls Working in Banks

Girls working in banks wear bouffant hair and shed
In their passage over the rather magnificent floors
Tiny shreds of perforated paper, like body flakes.
They walk through rows of youngish vice-presidents
With faraway looks, who dandle pencils and tend to
        ignore
The little tigerish lights flashing on their telephones.
When the girls return to their stations behind a friendly
        grid

They give out money neatly or graciously take it,
For not far from them the great interior glow of a vault
Built out of beaten dimes, stands open, shines,
Beaming security without ostentation.
If you glance inside it, there's nothing to be seen
But burnished drawers and polished steel elbows
Of the great machine of the door. It's a speckless world
With nobody inside it, like the best room in the gallery
Awaiting the picture which is still in a crate.
The girls change places frequently, moving their own
    addresses
From Open to Closed, Next Counter, or they walk away
With surprising freedom behind a wall or rise up on
    escalators
Past aging and well-groomed guards whose pistols seem
Almost apologetic as they watch people
Bending over Formica stand-up desks writing
With ballpoint pens attached to rosary chains,
After which the people select a queue in which they stand
Pious, abashed at the papery transactions,
And eventually walk with the subtlest sense of relief
Out of revolving doors into the glorious anonymous
    streets.

California Petrarchan

I hear the sunset ambulances surround
Suburbia at the turquoise edge of day,
Loping along the not-too-far freeway
Where olive trees and red bloodshed abound.

The oleanders with a shore-like sound
Perform their dance beside my own driveway
As if they also had a word to say
In all their whiteness beautifully gowned.

This Italy with insanity all its own
Lacks only history to make it true
And bitterness that ripens hour by hour.
This baby Italy, more straw than stone,
Stumbling, choking, fighting toward the New,
Bursts into flame with its own fire power.

Garage Sale

Two ladies sit in the spotless driveway
Casually smoking at the not-for-sale card table,
Over their heads a row of plastic pennants,
Orange, yellow, assorted reds and blues,
Such as flap over used-car lots, a symbol.
Each thing for sale is hand-marked with a label,
And every object shows its homemade bruise.

They sit there all day, sometimes getting up
When a visitor asks a question about a crib
Or a box spring with a broken rib
Or a gas jet to start fireplace fires.

Cars park gently, some with daisy decals,
No Mark IV's, Coupe de Villes or Corvettes;
Mostly wagons with the most copious interiors,
And few if any intellectuals.

All day the shoppers in low-key intensities,
Hoping to find something they are trying to remember
Fits in, or sticks out, approach and mosey,
Buy a coffee mug with a motto, or leave,
And nobody introduces him or herself by name.
That is taboo. And nobody walks fast. That is taboo.
And those who come look more or less the same.

A child buys a baby dress for her Raggedy Anns.
A pair of andirons, a mono hi-fi, a portable
    typewriter, square electric fans,
Things obsolescing but not mature enough to be
    antiques,
And of course paintings which were once expensive
Go or can go for a song.

This situation, this neighborly implosion,
As flat as the wallpaper of Matisse
Strikes one as a cultural masterpiece.
In this scene nothing serious can go wrong.

My Father's Funeral

Lurching from gloomy limousines we slip
On the warm baby-blanket of Baltimore snow,
Wet flakes smacking our faces like distraught
Kisses on cheeks, and step upon the green
Carpet of artificial grass which crunches
Underfoot, as if it were eating, and come
To the canopy, a half-shelter which provides

A kind of room to enclose us all, and the hole,
And the camp chairs, and following after,
The scrolly walnut coffin
That has my father in it.

Minutes ago in the noncommittal chapel
I saw his face, not looking himself at all
In that compartment hinged to open and shut,
A vaudeville prop with a small waxen man,
"So cold," the widow said and shied away
In a wide arc of centrifugal motion,
To come again to stand like me beside,
In the flowerless room with electric candelabra.
If there is among our people any heaven,
We are rather ambiguous about it
And tend to ignore the subject.

The rabbi's eulogy is succinct,
Accurate and sincere, and the great prayer
That finishes the speech is simply praise
Of God, the god my father took in stride
When he made us learn Hebrew and shorthand,
Taught us to be superior, as befits
A nation of individual priests.
At my sister's house we neither pray nor cry
Nor sit, but stand and drink and joke,
So that one of the youngsters says
It's more like a cocktail party.

For Dylan's dandy villanelle,
For Sylvia's oath of damnation one reserves
A technical respect. To Miller's Willie

And Lewis's Babbitt I demur.
My father was writing a book on salesmanship
While he was dying; it was his book of poems,
Destined to be unpublished. He hadn't time
To master books but kept the house well stocked
With random volumes, like a ship's library,
Rows and rows of forgotten classics,
Books for the sake of having books.

My father in black knee-socks and high shoes
Holding a whip to whip a top upstreet;
My father the court stenographer,
My father in slouch hat in the Rockies,
My father kissing my mother,
My father kissing his secretary,
In the high-school yearbook captioned Yid,
In synagogue at six in the morning praying
Three hundred and sixty-five days for his mother's rest,
My father at my elbow on the bimah
And presiding over the Sabbath.

In the old forgotten purlieus of the city
A Jewish ghetto in its day, there lie
My father's father, mother and the rest,
Now only a ghetto lost to time,
Ungreen, unwhite, unterraced like the new
Cemetery to which my father goes.
Abaddon, the old place of destruction;
Sheol, a new-made garden of the dead
Under the snow. Shalom be to his life,
Shalom be to his death.

My Fame's Not Feeling Well

My fame's not feeling well;
Maybe I should get it a Fulbright
To Luxembourg or Mexico,
Or maybe send it to a doctor-critic:
The doctor will say: "It should join a committee
Or win a national prize
Or judge a contest or apologize
For something, or just crawl out of its shell.
There's really nothing I can recommend."

Maybe I'll send it to Chicago where
A cabdriver once recognized it
Driving to O'Hare.

On the other hand I'd rather let it ail,
Being quite certain that it cannot fail
And simply come to an oblivious end.
Maybe it only needs a famous friend.

All the same it is slightly diabetic
And drinks more than its share of dry white wine,
But takes its dyazide and reserpine.

Sloth, acedia, ennui, otiose pride
Got it into this fix, so let it be.
I'm not the one to take its history.

To Lesbia

My Lesbia, let us live and love
And value at a penny's worth
The common leers and libels of
Old men and all their gamy mirth.

Suns may go down and rise again;
For us when once life's sudden light
Has fallen, what sleep comes on us then?
The sleep of one unbroken night.

Kiss me a thousand kisses, sweet,
To these a thousand thousand add,
And all these thousands then repeat
That none may know the sum we've had.

The best way to confuse these fools
Is to keep kissing while they count
Till they no longer know the rules
By which our mouths and bodies—mount!

(Catullus translation)

W.H.A.

Without him many of us would have never happened
But would have gone on being Georgians or worse;
We all recall how he galloped into verse
On Skelton's nag and easily reopened

Eighteenth-century prosody like a can of worms,
And there like Alice on a checkerboard
Careened through Marx and Freud and Kierkegaard
Dazzled and dazzling all the ideas and forms,

And camped out in the United States to wrinkle
Like an Indian squaw to await the Nobel Prize
And study savages with paleface eyes
And sit on Oxford Dictionaries and rankle.

God bless this poet who took the honest chances;
God bless the live poets whom his death enhances.

The Accountant

We went to him because we thought
    He was a Jew. His name was Low,
Wasn't it? And we were ushered in-
    To the presence of a tall and courtly
Chinese man, whose office over-
    Looked what seemed the entire West.

Each year we pay our ceremonial
    Visit for the W 2.
This doesn't take much time although
    The visit lasts the accountable hour
In which we discuss our families,
    Education, politics, in that order.
One thinks there should be tea perhaps,
    But no, only the ceremonious
Fifty-minute hour passed
    Pleasantly till we are done,
The accountant rises and we are led
    Back to the blond receptionist
Where we shake hands and smile and say
    Goodbye, good luck, until next year.

Mozart's Jew

Much as I enjoy your minor immortality, Da Ponte, I
marvel where you lie. New Jersey; New York;
something like that. My God, Da Ponte, you gave
Mozart the words for all that music. And why do
you make me uneasy? Because you were a Jew,
Emanuele Conegliano? Because you were a Cath-
olic priest, harried from town to town, country to
country, for your love affairs? Because you lie
and cover up in your book, only to be caught red-
handed? What difference does it make. You
called yourself a poet, you fraud, but you had
guts. Writing three plays for three different com-
posers at once, and one of them Mozart. And his
the *Don Giovanni*! Writing twelve hours on end,
like a Hollywood hack. And plenty of Tokay on
the table (*goût de terroir*) and lots of Seville to-
bacco, not to mention the sixteen-year-old girl,
your mistress during this project. I like you Da
Ponte. And finally bounced out of Europe itself,
to open a grocery store in New Jersey, that's al-
most too much. And failing at it, of course. And
yet I think you must have been the first to say of
Mozart: the greatest composer, past, present and
future. That little bit took genius to say. And the
Emperor Joseph liked you. And Casanova, jailed
for reading Voltaire. All of you Don Giovannis I
like, and you especially, Mozart's Jew, Da Ponte.

At Auden's Grave

From Vienna it's picture postcard all the way.
Where else on earth is such a land at ease!
The fat farms glistening, the polished pigs,
Each carven window box disgorging red
Geraniums, pencil pines and chestnut trees,
The gaily painted tractor rigs,
Steeples with onion domes that seem to say
Grüss Gott, come lie here in our flowerbed.

How many times did Auden take this train
Till that bright autumn day when he was borne
Back in a baggage car after his last
Recital, back to his Horatian house,
His cave of making, now the mask outworn,
The geographical visage consummated,
Back to the village, home to the country man
Without a country, home to the urban bard
Without a city he could call his own.

But suddenly a startling word
Leaps from the signpost of the country lane,
It's AUDENSTRASSE—
The poet becomes a street, the street a poet,
English with German music mated.

Here will arrive no pilgrim mob
As in Westminster Abbey, where his name
Is chiseled next to Eliot's. The sole cab
Has never heard of Auden, has to ask
Gasthaus directions, but we find him there
Ten yards away and settled with his slab,
The bracketed dates, the modest designation,
His plot planted to suffocation
In the country style of *horror vacui*.

Close by, a granite soldier stands
Bareheaded, bowed, without a gun,
Wearing his empty cartridge belt,
A blunt reminder of the First World War,
Signed *Unseren Helden* for those villagers
Who never returned and lay somewhere in France
Entre deux guerres before the next
World War should be begun
By the ultimate twentieth century hun.

Far from his foggy isle
The poet rests in self-exile.
Earth of the great composers of the wordless art
Enshrouds this master of the English tune
Not many miles from where Beethoven scrawled his will
When he could no longer hear the trill
Of the little yellow-hammer, nor the titanic storm.
In such a place Dame Kind
Released the intellectual minstrel's form.

Across the *Audenstrasse* from the grave
A bee drops from the chestnut, sips the beer,
Brings back his image to me, on a day
I bought him a tin collapsible cup to sip
His whiskey from, on some Iowa train,
Knowing his dread of that vertiginous plain.
Now all is comfy in his delectable cave.
I scatter the bee and greet him with my lip.

Whatever commentators come to say—
That life was not your bag—Edwardian—
Misogynist—Greenwich Villager—
Drifter—coward—traitorous clerk—or you,
In your own language, genteel anti-Jew—
I come to bless this plot where you are lain,
Poet who made poetry whole again.

Sandwiched between two families Auden lies,
At last one of the locals, over his grave
A cross, a battle monument, and a name
History will polish to a shine.
Down in the valley hums the Autobahn,
Up here the poet lies sleeping in a vale

That has no exits. All the same,
Right on target and just in time
A NATO fighter rips open the skies
Straight over Auden's domus and is gone.

Vietnam Memorial

for Liz

It lies on its side in the grassy Mall
A capsized V, a skeletal
Half-sunken hull of a lost cause
Between the Washington Monument and the Capitol.

To see it you descend a downward path
And stare up at the blackened decks of names,
Army of names that holds this cenotaph
Shimmering in shadow in the fosse.

Topside you can hear children at their games,
Down in this trench there is no gab,
Someone lays flowers under a name that was,
Our eyes like seaworms crawl across the slab.

Coasting the fifty-thousand here who died,
We surface breathless, come up bleary-eyed.

And Now, the Weather . . .

The rain that ripens oranges
   Will turn to knifey snow
Up on the sawtooth mountains
   Which we can see below.

The rain that fells the almonds
    Will dust the deserts pale
Have intercourse with Denver
    And then will really sail

To Iowa and Nebraska
    And dump its crystal tons
On all its patriotic
    Motherloving sons

Will cross the Appalachians
    Clasp the industrial murk
And lusting for the Apple
    Layer—at last—New York.

Grant's Tomb Revisited

Something unkempt about it
As if the tomb itself were moribund,
Sepulchre of our own Napoleon,
Litter fluttering under the battleflags
And few white faces.
We've all seen better days,
Hiram Ulysses.
They say the neighborhood is in transition
And only the Hudson keeps an even keel.

The stocky tower rises dirtily,
Imperial, republican,
With sculptures all wrong for today.
I'm puzzled why you like this place.
Pose me under the big stone eagle
Amidst the sociological decay.

Who collared this mausoleum with bright tiles,
Flashing, swooping childwork of the age,
Leaping around like a Luna Park?
Take my picture under the Miró arch,
A neighborhood Miró, not so bad at that.

Let's go upstairs, that's what it's all about
Where only a single guard remains inside
And seems almost surprised to see
Only two visitors, not in a group.

"One million people turned out for the event
"Buildings all over the city draped in black
"Sixty thousand marchers up Broadway
"Stretched seven miles, the President
"Cabinet, Supreme Court, almost the entire Congress
"Ships on the Hudson fired a salute

And there below
The two monogamous crypts
Eight and a half tons each
From the days when there was no doubt
About the reciprocity of might,
The General on the left and Julia on the right.

Homewreck

By and large there is no blood,
Police reports to the contrary notwithstanding,
But lots of ichor, a few missing books,
A hasty and disproportionate money transaction
And a sudden enlargement of space.

Three parties form the usual cast,
One happy, one in a rage, and one in the wings,
A telephone rings and rings and rings,
Incinerators open and close and open
And the dramatis personae have all lost face

Though they themselves don't think so
Or try not to think so because the immediate public
Is immediately involved,
Greedy to know what kind of problem is solved
By a seriously departing suitcase.

The public waits for the party in the wings
Who is no longer incognito, who
Has achieved stardom in a matinee
And appears shyly to complete the play
And just as shyly is proferred—an ashtray.

The Back

One of the foremost organs of beauty
Especially in women, spaceful and pure
A sky of skin uninterrupted
By mountain-tops and grots
Swamps, fens, rocks, trees
And serpents in gardens: the back.

A roseate fragrance endews it
It gleams like an Australian moon
And is no moor of thatch and thorn
But a mile wide river of veldt
Mile-wide and fraction-deep like the Platte
Where no man lives, a lone terrain,
And luxuriates in itself
And is the very mirage of beauty
To which even whispering is audibly loud
And there are no antries.

On this small platonic continent
Let love graze.

Retirement

Something tells him he is off-limits
When he visits the old establishment, maybe for mail.
He still has his key, but it has a slippery feel.
A colleague gives him a startled look, an over-emphatic
    Hi!
Both act almost as if they'd seen a ghost,
Both know they would rather meet on the street
Than in this particular environment, why
Meeting like this is a kind of misstep.
They wave each other off like a gardener and a bee.
Leaving, he stumbles a little, out of deference,
Hoping he won't run into any Young Turks
(Conversation with them is impossible,
    All idiom and no style).
Meanwhile he keeps coming back to the shop,
A distant cousin, a visitor, a janitor
Whose name is growing harder to recollect.
The word 'posthumous' pops into his head!
Has he joined some sect of the living dead?
After all, he's not some Supreme Court Judge
With unlimited tenure.
Besides, he cherishes his own retirement
And is working at it full time, like a work of art,
Hoping it's nothing as foolish as a hobby
Or as sentimental as a Purple Heart.

The Old Horsefly

Unseasonable weather, says the commentator,
Seventy in Manhattan in December.
Flu bugs as big as pigeons, I advise.

I saw a bee buzzing a sidewalk florist
On Broadway under a wall of Christmas trees.

Eleven floors up in the too-warm livingroom
A horsefly dashes window to wall and back,
A horsefly in December in Manhattan,
Off-course like those venturesome seagulls
Flying between two rivers and two parks
When the wind is right.
                            I get the flyswatter.

No entomologist, I decide
This is an old horsefly. I'll let it go,
Or is it a gadfly from the hotel row
Where carriage horses from another world
Still nod and stomp and swish their horsehair tails?

Its flight is frantic but I know that flies
That find their way in windows never find
The exit. I watch it speeding to and fro,

Disappearing, exploring other rooms
Till tired it lights on a white-painted door.

Biped approaches, raises his wand, then strikes.
Did I get it? I feel a pang—of what?

Whitman

Like Queen Victoria, he used the regal *we*,
Meaning the disciples of *Leaves of Grass*,
The American Bible they literally believed;
Sat by the hour to photographers,
The Open Shirt frontispiece,
The Good Gray, the Jesus, the Laughing Philosopher,
The Old Poet in the crumpled highcrown hat
Gazing in rapture at the butterfly
        Perched upon his forefinger
(It turns out was a cardboard butterfly);
To Tennyson the greatest of his time,
Inviting Walt to sail to the Isle of Wight;
Our first and probably our only guru,
Whose opinion of niggers (his designation) was low,
But worshipped Lincoln, to whom he scribed
        His second greatest song;
Who opened the Closet but wouldn't come out;
Who lived in a kind of luxurious poverty,
Housekeeper, male nurse, amanuensis, carriage,
        On the bounty of admirers,
Adored as Gandhi or a Dr. Schweitzer,

Visited by Oscar Wilde and English titles,
	In Camden, New Jersey;
Two hundred pounds of genius and hype,
Nature-mystic who designed his tomb
Solid as an Egyptian pyramid,
American to the soles of his boots,
Outspoken as Christ or Madame Blavatsky,
Messiah, Muse of the Modern, Mother!

Kleenex

Without kleenex how could we cry,
How could we let our hair down?
This box of veils reduces us to tears,
These tissues folding and unfolding hands.
The bottom of the box is an empty grave.
The gossamer kleenex is our comforter.
Here, says the psychiatrist, without saying *here*,
This soft note-paper for your complaint,
A throwaway in a throwaway world,
Spouses, children, lovers, jobs,
To cleanse one of one's ex,
Leaf within leaf a post-darwinian flower
Imperceptibly scented,
Transition to transition, mild as lettuce,
Smarmy as money with its lustful swish,
Epidermally virgin,
Kissing, dabbing our fears away.

Creative Writing

English was in its autumn when this weed
Sprang up on every quad.
The Humanities had long since gone to seed,
Grammar and prosody were as dead as Aztec.
Everyone was antsy except the Deans
Who smelled Innovation, Creativity!
Even athletes could take Creative Writing:
No books, no tests, best grades guaranteed,
A built-in therapy for all and sundry,
Taking in each other's laundry.
No schedule, no syllabus, no curriculum,
No more reading (knowledge has gone elsewhere).
Pry yourself open with a speculum
And put a tangle in your hair.

It spread from graduate school to kindergarten,
It moved to prisons, to aircraft carriers,
Competing with movies, blackjack and craps.
Civil war flared up from time to time
When real professors decided to weed the Grove,
Insecticide the pest, but the creative seed,
Stronger than gonorrhea or the med-fly,
Bounced down the highways like a tumbleweed,
Took to the air and the ocean seas,
Mated in Paris with the fleur-de-lis.

Ovid

For David Slavitt

Who would believe, in the sere and yellow leaf
    Of the twentieth century, that a white-haired poet
Could sit reading a translation of Ovid's *Tristia*
    With tears running down his face? Is it Alzheimer's
Or plain American narcissism such as dissolves a stadium
    Of football fans erect for *God Bless America*?
Poet who resurrected this rather ostracized classic:
    Question, Why did you? and second question,
Why does it hit me so hard? Are all poets exiles?
    What is it about this Ovid who got caught in the act,
The act of writing a love manual, and the act of the
        watcher?
    You strike a spark that leaps two thousand years
Like striking a match, and *eheu*! "smoke gets in your
        eyes."
    (Ovid wasn't as vulgar as that but then
He didn't live in PA or CA in the nineteen-nineties.)

What's more, your poem sets up sympathetic vibrations
    I never knew existed, say, Stesichorus,
Who supposedly wrote a poem in which he blamed Helen
    For the Trojan War and so incensed the Greeks
They blinded him, whereupon (too late) he recanted
    And wrote a poem about Helen the housewife,
Your attractive suburban type, and started the minor
        genre,

The poem of retraction, in which he denied that Helen
Ever left home. Posterity gives this the horse-laugh,
    Needing its femmes fatales, its white goddesses
And Ovid's court dollies. We groan at his retraction,
    And Dan Chaucer's palinode, and Herrick and Donne,
All lusty poets who slid back into *mea culpa*.
    It takes an American, Thoreau for instance, to say
If I have anything to regret, it's my good behavior.
    Not that I like Thoreau or any of those
Self-righteous prigs who think they're too pure to pay
        taxes.
    What you bring back is the Ovid of no solution
In your soul-torn book, the poet as he is and always was.

July 7, 1978

for Sophie

You marked the day
that, sitting in a tired chair,
gazing toward the exhausted light
white and silent as the telephone
it came to you, that ray,

why scamp it, that annunciation
hundreds of masters tried to paint,
the flêche d'amour that marks the way
from the quotidian penitentiary
to your epiphany.

Jacob Boehme saw it in a ray
that struck a pewter pot,
Whitman saw it where he lay
outstretched on the uncut hair of graves.
It came to you
wholly unbidden from your inner day.

Future-Present

Remember the old days when the luxury liners in
    narrow Manhattan
appeared piecemeal in segments at the end of east-west
    streets,
a black-and-white section of portholes and stripes of
    decks
and slowly the majesty of the great red funnel,
even the olympian basso of its homing horn?
It would take a full half hour to go past,
as if in no hurry to pass into history.

But look there at the top pane of the window!
A burnished skyliner elegantly moving north,
as proud as leviathan above the suffering Hudson,
past the unfinished cathedral, over Grant's tomb,
into the blue-gray morning of the future-present.

"There's One"

In the village of board sidewalks, striped awnings,
Saturday's horses and the red clay river
South of Petersburg,
Grandpa presides in his dry-goods store,
Uncle Harry, about fourteen, is selling shoes,
Mother, behind the notions counter, is only a girl,
Grandpa in dark serge and beard
Is thumping and measuring bolts of cloth on the table.

A farmer in bib overalls with two young children,
A girl and a boy come into the cloth-smelling store.
The farmer stops and points to grandpa
In his dark serge and beard and says to the children,
There's one,
Then to my mother who is only a girl,
There's one, he says.

BIOGRAPHICAL NOTE

Karl Shapiro was born November 10, 1913, in Baltimore, Maryland, and attended schools in Baltimore, Chicago, and Virginia. After one year at the University of Virginia he dropped out and traveled to Tahiti; his first book, *Poems*, was published in 1935. After further study at Johns Hopkins and Enoch Pratt Library School in Baltimore, he was drafted into the army in 1941, ultimately serving with a medical unit in New Guinea. During his military service he wrote prolifically, publishing *Person, Place and Thing* (1942), which won *Poetry* magazine's Levinson Prize, *The Place of Love* (1942), the Pulitzer Prize–winning *V-Letter and Other Poems* (1944), and *Essay on Rime* (1945). He served as Consultant in Poetry at the Library of Congress, 1946–47; was named associate professor of writing at Johns Hopkins (1947); and edited *Poetry* (1950–56) and the *Newberry Library Bulletin* (1953–56). In 1956 he became professor at the University of Nebraska and editor of *Prairie Schooner*; he subsequently taught at the University of Chicago and the University of California at Davis. His later poetry was collected in *Trial of a Poet* (1947), *Poems of a Jew* (1958), *The Bourgeois Poet* (1964), *Selected Poems* (1968), *White-Haired Lover* (1968), *Adult Bookstore* (1976), *Collected Poems*

1940–1978 (1978), *The Old Horsefly* (1992), and *The Wild Card* (1998). His essays were collected in *In Defense of Ignorance* (1960), *To Abolish Children* (1968), and *The Poetry Wreck* (1975); he also published a novel, *Edsel* (1971), and two volumes of an autobiography, *The Younger Son* (1988) and *Reports of My Death* (1990). He died on May 14, 2000, in New York City.

NOTE ON THE TEXTS

The texts of the poems in this volume are taken from *Collected Poems 1940–1978* (New York: Random House, 1978), except for works not included in that edition. The texts of poems that do not appear in *Collected Poems* are printed from the following sources:

"My Hair," "The Tongue": *The Place of Love* (Melbourne, Australia: Comment Press, 1942).

"Aside," "Birthday Poem," "Movie," "Crusoe," "Spider": *V-Letter and Other Poems* (New York: Reynal & Hitchcock, 1944).

from *Essay on Rime*: *Essay on Rime* (New York: Reynal & Hitchcock, 1945). Line numbers in the margins of the source text have not been reproduced in the present edition.

"Demobilization," "An Urn of Ashes," from "Recapitulations," "Words for a Child's Birthday," "Air Liner," from "Trial of a Poet": *Trial of a Poet* (New York: Reynal & Hitchcock, 1947). "Recapitulations" is included in *Collected Poems* in shortened form, omitting two sections reprinted in the present volume.

"War Movies" ["#37"]: *The Bourgeois Poet* (New York: Random House, 1964). Title supplied for this volume (see Introduction, xxviii-xxix).

"You Played Chopin," "How Do I Love You?" "O My Beloved": *White-Haired Lover* (New York: Random House, 1968).

"My Fame's Not Feeling Well," "To Lesbia": *Adult Bookstore* (New York: Random House, 1976).

"At Auden's Grave," "Vietnam Memorial," "And Now, the Weather . . . ," "Grant's Tomb Revisited," "Homewreck," "The Back," "Retirement": *New & Selected Poems 1940–1986* (Chicago: University of Chicago Press, 1987).

"The Old Horsefly," "Whitman," "Kleenex," "Creative Writing," "Ovid," "July 7, 1978," "Future-Present," "There's One": *The Old Horsefly* (Orono, Me.: Northern Lights, 1992).

This volume corrects the following typographical errors in the source texts, cited by page and line number: 41.25, tighten; 43.18, Soft-minded; 164.20, poety.

The following is a list of pages where a stanza break coincides with the foot of the page (except where such breaks are apparent from the regular stanzaic structure of the poem): 116, 142, 154, 163, 164, 167, 177.

NOTES

6.2–3   *I do remember . . . 'a dwells*]   *Romeo and Juliet*, V.i.37–38.

16.9   Gargantua]   Omnivorous protagonist of François Rabelais' *Grandes et Inestimables Chroniques du grand et énorme géant Gargantua* (1532).

18.13   the true nobleman]   Thomas Jefferson, who founded the University of Virginia in 1819.

35.1   Giantess]   Translation of "La Géante" by Charles Baudelaire.

47.4   Curtis]   Cyrus Curtis (1850–1933), Philadelphia-based publisher who founded *Ladies' Home Journal*, *Saturday Evening Post*, and *Philadelphia Inquirer*, among other publications.

47.12   His wife whom sleeping Milton thought he saw]   Cf. John Milton, Sonnet 23: "Methought I saw my late espousèd saint/Brought to me like Alcestis from the grave."

51.13   Judenhetze]   Jew-baiting.

52.6   Rahab]   Harlot of Jericho who concealed Israelite spies, and was spared with her family after the Israelite conquest of the city (cf. Joshua 2:1–6:25).

53.16   Anna]   The protagonist of Tolstoy's *Anna Karenina*.

61.14–15   *on mourrait . . . industriels?*]   One would die for the industrial workers?

65.2   *What should . . . jigging fools?*]   *Julius Caesar*, IV.iii.137.

66.27   *l'homme qui rît*]   The man who laughs; title of a novel (1869) by Victor Hugo.

67.2   Arachne]   A skilled weaver, she vied unsuccessfully with Athena and hanged herself, after which the goddess changed her into a spider.

74.1   Dorian Gray] Decadent, miraculously youthful protagonist of Oscar Wilde's novel *The Picture of Dorian Gray* (1890).

74.5   "Fruits and flowers among"] Ernest Dowson, "Villanelle of the Poet's Road," line 16.

74.11   "Call us not tragic"] First line of the penultimate stanza of part XVII of *Look, Stranger!* (1936).

85.18   *To wicked spirits . . . assigned*] John Donne, "Holy Sonnet 13," line 13.

85.23   *Done is . . . dragon blak!*] William Dunbar, "On the Resurrection of Christ," line 1.

86.26   *Les Fleurs du Mal*] *The Flowers of Evil* (1857) by Charles Baudelaire.

94.3   "Colours of Good and Evil"] An addendum to Bacon's *Essays* (1597).

94.18   the fair Phrygian] The Phrygian cap—worn by ancient slaves upon gaining their freedom—was a symbol of liberty during the French Revolution.

96.3   As Columbus broke the egg] According to tradition, Columbus was asked at a banquet if he thought someone else would have discovered the New World had he not done so. In response, Columbus asked the guests to stand an egg on one end; when they failed, he crushed one end against the table and stood it on the flattened part.

107.22   The great biologist] T. H. Huxley (1825–95); "On a Piece of Chalk," originally delivered as a lecture, was first published in 1868.

125.7   *Tabu* by Murnau] Made partly in collaboration with Robert Flaherty, F. W. Murnau's last film (1931) was shot in Tahiti.

133.20–21   *Syntopicon*] Topical two-volume index to *The Great Books of the Western World* (1952), a library of classic works edited by Mortimer J. Adler and Robert Hutchins.

133.21   *The Harvard Classics*] A 50-volume series edited by Charles W. Eliot, president of Harvard, published in 1910; it was sometimes known as "Dr. Eliot's Five-Foot Shelf."

134.10–11   love one another or die] W. H. Auden, "September 1, 1939." Auden later changed the phrase to read "love one another and die."

139.23   Altamiras] Altamira, caverns in northern Spain where extensive prehistoric paintings were discovered in 1879.

148.12   *Et c'est la fin . . . ensemble*] "And that is the end for which we are together": cf. François Villon, *Le Testament*, "Ballade: Au poinct du jour que l'esprevier s'esbat."

152.15   The expense . . . shame] Cf. Shakespeare, Sonnet 129: "Th'expense of spirit in a waste of shame/Is lust in action."

156.27   Dylan's dandy villanelle]   "Do Not Go Gentle Into That Good Night" by Dylan Thomas.

156.28   Sylvia's oath of damnation]   "Lady Lazarus" by Sylvia Plath, collected in *Ariel* (1966).

156.29   Miller's Willie]   Willie Loman, protagonist of Arthur Miller's play *Death of a Salesman* (1949).

157.1   Lewis's Babbitt]   George F. Babbitt, real estate broker who is the protagonist of Sinclair Lewis's novel *Babbitt* (1922).

159.1   To Lesbia]   Cf. Catullus, *Carmina* V.

164.14   *Unseren Helden*]   Our heroes.

164.16   *Entre deux guerres*]   Between two wars.

168.9   Luna Park]   An amusement park at Coney Island, Brooklyn.

174.7   Madame Blavatsky]   Helena Petrovna Blavatsky (1831–91), Russian-born theosophist whose books included *Isis Unveiled* (1871) and *The Secret Doctrine* (1888).

176.3   sere and yellow leaf]   Cf. *Macbeth*, V.iii.23.

177.20   that ray]   In the words of a February 25, 2002, letter from Sophie Wilkins to the editor, "It refers to an epiphany of mine I told him of: That afternoon I was alone . . . and gazing out the sunset-window . . . it came to me that I could give up my lifelong wish to be someone else (better, more productive, more my true self whatever it was) it came to me, thus: All you need to be is just what you are, which nobody else can be."

INDEX OF TITLES
AND FIRST LINES

AMERICAN POETS PROJECT

EDNA ST. VINCENT MILLAY: SELECTED POEMS
J. D. McClatchy, editor
ISBN 1-931082-35-9 $20.00

POETS OF WORLD WAR II
Harvey Shapiro, editor
ISBN 1-931082-33-2 $20.00

KARL SHAPIRO: SELECTED POEMS
John Updike, editor
ISBN 1-931082-34-0 $20.00

WALT WHITMAN: SELECTED POEMS
Harold Bloom, editor
ISBN 1-931082-32-4 $20.00